I AM NO LONGER AFRAID TO DIE

WITNESS GAZA

AMIRA ALZANEEN
AND JEANNIE AMASH

TreeWater Initiative

Paperback ISBN-13: 979-8-9989743-1-1

Ebook ISBN-13: 979-8-9989743-0-4

Cover design and book promotion by Martha Stephens and Manlio Pertout
Book design and typesetting by Abbie Phelps
Text set in Adobe Garamond Pro and DM Sans

TreeWater Initiative

TABLE OF CONTENTS

FOREWORD
BY ROLAND BENNETT

On August 8th, 1933, my grandfather Paul Amash was born in Lydda, Palestine. At the age of fourteen, he became a refugee in what some call the 1948 Palestinian Expulsion from Lydda and Ramle and others call the Lydda Massacre or Lydda Death March. As a refugee in Ramallah, he obtained a scholarship to the Quaker Friends Boys' School there. Academia took him to the United States, to Juniata College, Pennsylvania State University, Elon College, and finally UNC Chapel Hill, where he earned his PhD in romance languages. He married my grandmother, Ann Amash, and they settled in Marietta, Ohio, where he was a professor at Marietta College. They had four children: Ed, my mother Jeannie, Caroline, and my namesake and uncle Roland.

In 2016, Paul passed away at the age of eighty-two. While grappling with the loss of her father, my mother felt a need to visit the land from which he came. A need to better understand not only him, but also herself. Knowing not a word of Arabic and having never been further east than France, my mother took off for the first of many trips to Palestine in January, 2017. She founded TreeWater Initiative, a nonprofit with the goal of planting a million seeds of hope in Palestine. Since then, she has helped Palestinian farmers, primarily by providing them with olive trees. She has also provided Palestinians in Gaza with microfinance grants to get their businesses off the ground.

This work led her to Amira Alzaneen of Gaza. Their meeting was random, over the telephone—someone could not understand my mom's English, so they called on Amira who happened to be there, to translate. They became close friends and communicated regularly through WhatsApp. In 2022, my mother was granted sponsorship from St. Porphyrius Greek Orthodox Church in Gaza and was able to enter Gaza for the first time; she and Amira were finally able to meet in person.

I do not need to tell you the events of October 7, 2023, and what followed. This book tells Amira's story—her experience of the bombings of her home in Gaza City, the Israeli ground invasion, her flight south to the sprawling refugee camps that formed outside of Rafah, the bombings and eventual invasion there, and so on, primarily through her WhatsApp messages with my mother.

My mom told me that she had taken screenshots of her and Amira's conversations and printed them out at the public library, and was going to write a book with them. She told me that she had voice messages from Amira as well that she was going to transcribe. I told her that my mother would never have to do that work. I got her to export their conversation data to me, wrote a script to parse through it and then wrote and compiled a LaTeX script into a PDF—and voila, my mother had a layout and beginning draft for her book.

There is a crushing hopelessness that consumes the Palestinian American. Of course, I am beyond thankful that I am safe in my home in New York and not being bombed. But to see our government endorse and aid the slaughter of our people and feel helpless to affect it breeds despair and depression. Calling our representatives, marching in the street, posting on social media—all of these give some feeling of agency, but as the genocide continues it is hard not to lose hope and fall more deeply into despair. I find some relief in helping elevate Amira's voice, hoping that reading this could help change the minds of my fellow Americans.

INTRODUCTION
BY JEANNIE AMASH

A friend in the West Bank called to tell me about a dream he had recently. He had dreamt of a golden angel with the name of God written across its chest. Golden sparkles emanated from the wings. People were screaming at the sight of the angel, but not with fear. This angel had no gender, and came for everyone. There was an evil happening, and this angel had come to overcome the evil. My friend said he usually forgot his dreams. This one stayed.

My friend, who lives in occupied Nablus in Palestine, has been subjected to many violent intrusions from the Israeli Offensive Forces. His father was jailed and tortured (with three fingers cut off); he himself was beaten by IOF soldiers when he was sixteen, as he walked to work one morning. His home was raided, his friends shot, relatives murdered—oh, the list is long. And still, my friend called to tell me of an angel come to accept everyone and overcome evil. He is a Palestinian.

I thought for a minute, then decided to open this book, which details horrors of Gaza, with his dream. Why? Because he said the angel had come for everyone. The golden, nongendered angel proclaiming the word God in Arabic had come for everyone.

In a world far more perfect than this one—and one I do imagine—everyone is covered by the sanctity of God, an angel, or some benevolent force more powerful than all the evil that has bestowed itself upon us.

* * *

In August 2018, I was with this very friend in a café in Nablus, having lunch on a beautiful sunny day. The waiters were his cousins, two brothers from Gaza. While we were having lunch, they called home to speak with another brother. Of course, the waiters told their brother about the American woman they were waiting on, and I was handed the phone. I don't speak Arabic; they did not speak any English. However, they were with a friend who did: a young woman named Amira Alzaneen.

So began another enduring friendship, Amira and I. The telephone conversation she translated in that café has long since been forgotten, but Amira and I exchanged numbers and continued our communication. Over the next few years, I got to know her, her family situation, her dreams and aspirations. She wrote to me often on various internet platforms. I recognized early on that she had a gift for writing. She had a persistence about her—a determination to tell her story, the stories of those around her, of Gaza. Even though her English was far from perfect, she worked at it. How often those stories, in the few short years between the summer of 2018 and October 7, 2023, were about the current bombings she and those she knew were enduring.

It is shocking to think that some people still think everything started on October 7. Israel claims it was the biggest day of slaughter since the Holocaust. What Israel fails to say is that that day still pales compared to the regular bombings that took place in Gaza before October 7, 2023. Amira wrote of bombings in 2019, 2020, 2021, and 2022.

Violence aside, while she wrote about the difficulty of her life in

Gaza, she also told me how she loved it. She described it as the most beautiful place on earth. It is also almost all she had ever known. She had never left Gaza until 2020, when she traveled to Egypt with her father so he could receive surgery for an Israeli bullet that had lodged near his spine during the second Intifada. My point here is not to document every incursion made by Israel into Gaza in my time of knowing Amira, but rather to let the reader here know that bombings have been part of her life, sometimes her daily life, since she was born.

I was granted a five-day permit to enter Gaza in December 2022. The bishop of St. Porphyrius Greek Orthodox Church had put in a request to Israel, and my permit was granted on fairly short notice. I was very lucky. I have relatives who are members of the church, and through them my desire to visit Gaza was made known to the bishop.

I had started a nonprofit in 2018 called the TreeWater Initiative, and with the assistance and commitment of a relative in the church, we had been able to carry out several meaningful projects in the Strip. One of those projects had been to build a roof over a sheep enclosure that was home to about fourteen sheep owned by Amira's father. We also provided their winter feed. With the priceless assistance of Ibrahim Amash, we had managed to complete this project plus the planting of about two hundred olive trees, as well as the financing and procurement of supplies for two rabbit-breeding businesses for single women heads of households. Because of this work and Ibrahim's family's steadfast involvement with the church, the bishop was willing to request my permit.

From an early morning departure from Ramallah to Jerusalem, to a long taxi ride across the country to Gaza, I arrived at the Erez Crossing in a taxi full of workers returning home from their shifts in Israel, along with one of my hosts, Tawfiq, who had met me in Jerusalem. As I arrived at the checkpoint, I was videotaping the separation wall, complete with barbed wire across the top. As I reviewed the video much later, I realized I had also recorded a conversation between some of the men. I listened carefully and heard the word *Hamas*. I sent it over to my friend to translate, and he told me they said: "The members of Hamas, they made it hard on us."

After the Israeli checkpoint, then the Hamas checkpoint, I finally passed through to a parked car where Ibrahim was waiting. Oh my God, my excitement, my shock, my wonderment. Here I was in that forbidden place I had longed to visit, for real. It was hot. The sky was tremendously blue. We drove. I videoed everything I could. I wished my brilliant videographer son had been with me—he could capture much better than I knew I would—but I did my best.

The poverty in the areas close to the border was immediately visible. This was Beit Hanoun, the closest border town to Israel, and one of the poorest areas. Because of its proximity to the wall, the residents here heard every rocket ever fired by Israel pass overhead. This was also Amira's town. Block after block of cement apartment buildings were unadorned, mostly gray, without paint to add beauty. The most color I observed in this area was from the graffiti, mostly Arabic script, on street-level walls. Some of the graffitied walls had been spray-painted in Arabic so many times that it would be hard to decipher any of it, peering through the layers of script. Some were newer. Those could be translated. One celebrated a wedding party, listing the names of the family. Another wished everyone a blessed Eid. Some were painted magnificently, the gorgeous script weaving around itself as works of art. Pastel orange-gold paint outlined in black. Red, green, black script, little blue embellishments. Some of these were not spray-painted; they were too precise. These were calligraphy wall art.

The windows were like dark rectangles in rows lining the building walls. If there was a balcony, there was usually laundry hanging on it. Many of the buildings, at street level, had the wide metal doors that opened like garage doors, lifting open from the sidewalks. Many shops in Palestine are like this. This Thursday morning, many were closed. I wasn't sure why the streets seemed empty. A lone woman walked here, then an adolescent boy, then another young girl. We passed a bare lot between buildings where children played. Some people sat in plastic chairs lined against shaded parts of the buildings.

As we drove, a few more people scattered the streets. There were a few cars, a few donkey-pulled carts riding in the street, and even a couple camels with their drivers perched on top. On other days, when we drove in the center of Gaza City, traffic would be fierce. Right alongside cars, in traffic, bumper to bumper and bumper to nose, were those donkeys pulling carts. I was entertained by this. It was so new to me. It all was.

They drove me to the sea. The Mediterranean Sea of Gaza is the bluest ocean I have ever seen. It is breathtakingly beautiful. There are places where the blue plays with green, rippling into teals and aquas, smoothing out into blue again. The Sea of Gaza.

The harbor was full of boats. They had already been out since before dawn and returned at dawn with their catch. The fisherman had already left the pier; on later days, when I arrived at 7:00 a.m., I would learn the early morning hours were filled with the fervent activities of hauling in the catch, cleaning fish, and laying fresh bounty out on blankets where customers haggled for their dinners. Young boys as well as grown men gutted and cleaned with blackened hands and sharp knives, and pier cats waited patiently for scraps thrown or dropped their way. (Those smart kitties had the life. Then.)

But these fishing boats were old, lacking in any fresh paint. Some seemed rickety; some were glorified rowboats. This was my first moment of astonishment—the first moment I experienced that feeling one gets as they go another step into the occupation. I'd had those moments many times in the West Bank. I had been through plenty of checkpoints. I had already walked through the poverty of refugee camps. But these rickety boats were all that were docked at the port of Gaza. These boats were how Gazans brought in the famous varieties of fish that are known all over Palestine. These were the boats where fishermen hand-cast their nets to the sea and hauled in the morning catch—the boats fishermen were shot in if they went too far out to sea and encountered Israeli Terrorist Forces patrolling the waters. There were no giant steamers, like the one I had seen when I was in Haifa.

I turned around and gazed at Gaza City. It was modern. It wasn't. Gray and white. Tall buildings, short buildings in concrete block. Occasional light browns. There was no colorful, elegant architecture playing against the sky. All I saw was cement block building after cement block building. Many were nearly as tall as other modern buildings would be, but utterly lacking in that wow effect. There were a few turrets I assumed belonged to mosques. Gaza was not a playground of modern architectural opportunity. It was a city built from necessity, and sometimes, as quickly as possible, from rubble.

Two days into my journey, I was driving back to Beit Hanoun with Ibrahim and his close friend Maysara, who was serving as translator, to meet Amira and her family for the first time. When we arrived, Amira wasn't home yet, so we were taken by her mother to visit the roof over the sheep enclosure TreeWater Initiative had built. It was located on the side of the lane just down from their house, crowded between other structures, and I was left to wonder where the sheep went when they left their enclosure.

Amira arrived a few minutes later. It was a joyous moment. We embraced. We went back to the house, where we all sat and talked.

It was not an easy conversation. Her family was evidently very poor. The walls had not been painted in years. The furniture was old. From this simple place had come this wonderfully ambitious daughter. Amira, her mother Siham, Maysara, and I engaged in a vigorous conversation about Amira and her future. Siham spoke no English. Amira spoke well enough. Ibrahim sat across the room, sometimes with his head on his hand as he endured this conversation between women. Amira's sister Warda sat on the other side of the room, feeding her baby from a small cup. Osama, Amira's brother, was close in age to her, a tall and striking young man with a chiseled jaw; he came in smiling and began cooing to the baby. I knew of Osama from previous conversations with Amira. He had been shot in his right calf by an Israeli sniper during the Great March of Return in Gaza in 2018. He had been unarmed. The bullet had been a butterfly bullet, meaning that it expanded upon impact with flesh. I had seen photos of his injury. His lower leg had looked like ground hamburger. Later he showed me his healed but deeply scarred calf.

Here we had Amira the outlier. She was a young woman, only twenty-five at that time. She wrote. She dreamed. She wanted nothing more than to go back and finish her university degree. She was determined to become a translator, a writer, something that would make use of her love of language, writing, and poetry. Amira's parents had no higher education. Although Amira was able to imagine a better life for herself, and was willing to work for it, her mom, though clearly intelligent and strong, could not see beyond a life of marriage and children. As I explained that Amira had a special gift, Siham would respond that all of her children were special, and Amira not more than any of them.

I don't like using the word *special* when I describe people, and of course no one child is more special than another, no matter what their talents may be. But I was not able to help Siham understand before we left that Amira had an ambition beyond the life right in front of her. Her mom had only known this life, accepted it for herself and her children, and could or would not envision something different for Amira. The divide it caused was tremendous. At this juncture, Amira was fighting for her right to continue her education. She did manage to get back into Palestine University again, and was a couple semesters shy of graduating before October 7. It is important to mention here that the literacy rate in Gaza and the West Bank is close to 98 percent, higher than in the United States.

We took photos together—me with Amira, her mom, and her brother Osama. We said our goodbyes, and Ibrahim, Maysara, and I continued on to the next project: another impoverished family in Beit Hanoun that had been the recipient of one of the rabbit-breeding initiatives. In this case, the single mother was breeding these rabbits to pay for her oldest daughter to go to college—a completely different mindset. It is dangerous to judge, or lump people into one category.

My impressions and experiences of and in Gaza could fill another book. What is important here is to begin the story of Amira's journey through a genocide with a background of where she started. I believe the astute reader will find nuances over and over again that pertain to how much the normalization of Israeli terror permeated daily life.

* * *

With all its poverty and all its concrete block, Gaza was still a beauty filled place full of life. Through every blockade, every bombing, the life and love of Gaza was still there. A hard life, but still, a life. The beaches were too beautiful, the sky too blue, the energy too vibrant. Did people long for more freedom? Yes. Was it bewildering at first when I was told by some people that if I heard the sound of overhead drones or even a bomb, not to worry? Was it utterly annoying to have limited electricity to the point of women staying up sometimes in the middle of the night because it was the only time they could run their washing machines? Annoying that bottled water had to be used for drinking water because Israel had appropriated so much of the ground water under Gaza that it was too saline to drink. My showers had a salty taste if water got in my mouth. Did it feel like being in the twilight zone to be driven to multiple neighborhoods that had previously been completely leveled by Israeli bombs to see that they had been immediately rebuilt? To realize how much funding it took to be constantly rebuilding? Was it sad that to come in or out of Gaza for most people was impossible unless they had a permit issued by Israel? And even then you had to go through the rigors of a heartless checkpoint every time. Travel beyond those tiny borders was impossible for most. I had tried for years to get that one-time five-day permit. I often hear Gaza referred to as an open air prison. I cringe a bit because although that description fits what Israel has tried to make it, it doesn't fit what Gazans had made of it. They did manage to find joy in their lives. They loved, they laughed, they bled, they died within those walls just like every other group of humans. I was welcomed profusely. I was served lovely meals. I was waved to and flashed peace signs by waiters in open to the street restaurants, by men driving rickety looking trailers ingeniously piled 10 feet high with just about anything and being pulled by those donkeys. I was smiled at, thrown kisses to by children. Where was all this fear I was supposed to feel as a clearly non Gazan woman, walking around sometimes by myself? I was living through the myths of Gaza being dangerous to foreigners, especially a non hijab wearing woman walking around by herself. I also was living through the myth that Israel was not aggressive and oppressive. They did bomb neighborhoods illegally under international law. Families had become accustomed to having loved ones die during those bombings. Parents had learned how to console their children during air raids to quell their fears while trying not to show their own.

My father, Dr. Paul J. Amash, was born in Lydda, Palestine, in 1933. His mother, Regina, bore eleven children. Eight survived into adulthood. My grandfather, Jirius, was involved with the church. I have heard he was a deacon, a minister, but I am not actually sure. I have heard that he had an astounding memory. They were villagers.

When I was growing up, my father would hold me and my three siblings rapt as we listened to his brilliant storytelling around the dinner table. Most of the stories were about the shenanigans of different characters of Palestinian village life. Woven into the stories were images of urns of olives, preserved in oil from their trees; Jaffa oranges succulent enough that you could poke a straw into one and suck out the fresh juice. Without those stories, I would have had no idea of Palestine but for the nightly news. Our home contrasted the hilarious characters of Palestinian village life with the tragic, propagandized portrayal of Palestinians in the media.

The Nakba, the forced displacement of nearly a million Palestinians by the Zionist forces, happened when my father was fourteen years old. He walked.

His displacement came in July of 1948. It is referred to historically as the Death March of Lydda. He was forced from his village to walk in the intense July heat for miles with his family, and tens of thousands of others. All of them left with nothing. His walk ended in a refugee camp in Ramallah, in the West Bank of Palestine. Others went to Nablus, Gaza, Lebanon. There are Palestinian refugee camps all over the Middle East. I can certainly say that every one of them, refugees forced from their homes, lands, communities, carried the same shock of displacement and betrayal.

My father was never able to talk about what happened in any rational conversation with me. My knowledge came from stories my American mom told me, stories that came from other members of his family who had walked. They are all horrifying, barbaric, cruel. There was one time though, when I was about twelve years old. I remember I was thirsty, maybe even whining a little bit about needing a glass of water. Out of nowhere, my father began yelling at me. "Thirsty? You are thirsty? When we walked we had no water. My aunt urinated into a cup and gave it to my cousin and said, 'Here! Drink.'" I remember looking into his eyes and witnessing a raging pain for a few seconds. I was stunned into silence. It took me a long time to recognize that, as brilliant as my father truly was—a distinguished linguistic scholar who spoke seven languages, taught in universities internationally, was an expert on the Bible and the Koran, and as a child who spoke English and French so well that British soldiers used him as a translator—was never able to relieve his trauma, or fully express his brilliance in the United States amongst his peers. His being a Palestinian in the USA carried a heartless prejudice that he personally found difficult to overcome.

In spite of all of this, my father and many members of his immediate and extended family achieved great success in the United States. I am immensely proud of their achievements. They have made enormous contributions in many diverse fields including politics, law, business/entrepreneurship, academia, and teaching, to name a few.

One thing my father did say to me about his life before the Nakba was, "We didn't fight. We worked side by side." Meaning, of course, all the inhabitants of Palestine . . . Christians, Muslims, and Jews.

Though we still hear about the horrors of the Holocaust in Europe, which had just preceded this Nakba by a few short years, the survivors of the Nakba had no outlets to express or validate their experiences. An ingenious system of propaganda quickly permeated society, leading people to believe that Palestinians were terrorists and every violent act committed against Israel unprovoked. It still amazes me how many people still fall for this narrative. But what amazes me even more today are the numbers of people that are seeing beyond it. These are the champions of the world today.

People are standing up for Palestine who have no direct connection to the land. Youth on college campuses are risking their education to speak the truth. They are being beaten and then portrayed as violent. The propaganda machine is in full force, calling out anyone, including Jews, as anti-Semitic. Jews who speak up for Palestine are labeled as self-hating. Nothing could be further from the truth.

Imagine your life today if you were to suddenly hear the sounds of bombs flying overhead. Explosions. Would you grab your phone and start recording within the first minute? And then send those recordings to a friend immediately? I doubt it. I imagine you would be panicking in utter confusion. But for someone in Gaza, this was commonplace. Although it was not known at the time what was happening, Amira had so much experience living with bombs that she did start recording, and sending messages, all morning, to me. Even though she had become used to it, it still did not stop the sound of her terrified breath coming through the noise of the explosions.

When those first bombs were cast by Hamas on October 7, in the chaos that ensued, I knew—I absolutely knew—that the next retaliation by Israel would be a slaughter bigger than anything seen thus far in Gaza. I practically begged people to understand what was coming and to speak up to stop it. And the responses I got were . . . that I was a Hamas supporter. That Israel had a right to defend itself. That people couldn't talk to me because I was a Hamas supporter. People wrote that Palestine didn't exist, that Palestine had been given to Israel by the British Mandate. That Palestinians have turned down every peace agreement offered to them. (A side note on that particular topic—I would lay down money that not a single person who threw that argument in my face knew any of the details of what those so-called peace agreements entailed.)

I knew that the terrible tragedy that had just occurred on October 7, 2023, was going to be used as a justification to create an even greater one. It has been.

* * *

Amira kept communicating with me during October 7 and beyond. Because she lived in Beit Hanoun on the border, I knew she was in imminent, immediate danger. All I knew to do as I watched from afar was to tell her to write to me.

Write to me, Amira. Write about this. And write she did. I left most of her English as she wrote it and spoke it unless small changes were needed for clarification.

She wrote while sitting in her destroyed home. She wrote as she went through the first, almost immediate round of colleagues and family being murdered. She wrote about family being bombed a few feet away from her. She was in Al Shifa Hospital. She made the flight to Rafah. She lived through it all; she kept recording her experiences, and she kept sending them to me.

Amira is a Superhero.

Through her eyes, I invite you to witness Gaza.

INTRODUCTION
BY AMIRA ALZANEEN
أميرة الزعانين

After the release of my high school results for the year 2015, I passed it with a good grade, and despite my family's bad circumstances, which may not enable me to study at the university and afford its expenses, I did not give up and began the journey of searching and registering at the university. I aspired to study language translation, a specialty that I could not find in the universities of Gaza. I have loved writing for many years, reciting poetry, etc., so the major I was closest to was studying media and communication, and I registered at the University of Palestine for a bachelor's degree.

I was very enthusiastic and had a great passion and love for practice and learning. The teachers loved my energy and diligence and this great enthusiasm, and I applied what I studied at the university in a direct practical way and it grew. This is my ability to write and create more and more broadly, and my understanding and information increased. I studied for about a year and a half, three semesters, which I finished with an excellent and very good grade. I had a small job as a secretary in an office through which I could pay some of my university fees.

However, a catastrophe happened to me that changed the course of my life. In 2018, my eldest brother Osama was injured in his leg during the return marches by the occupation. He was the breadwinner for our family due to my father's illness and his suffering from a bullet in his back since the intifada that prevented him from working. Our lives began to get worse and worse, and we looked for all ways to treat Osama and I was then forced to leave the university and postpone it. My classes were due to the accumulation of fees, the inability to provide what was needed, the great needs of the house, and the search for additional work so that I could support them. Osama was subjected to many operations in Gaza, most of which were unsuccessful, and there was a fear of his foot being amputated. It was decided for him to travel to Egypt to begin a full medical journey. It was never that easy, as it was forbidden for anyone of his age to go out without coordination, which at the time cost an exorbitant sum estimated at $1,400 per person, in addition to housing, treatment, and transportation expenses. My mother traveled with him to support him and relieve him, and I became responsible for the house, including what was in it, and to support my eight brothers and sisters.

I stopped studying for two years. But I did not give up. I still had a dream to finish it and obtain the university degree that most of my generation had preceded me. During Osama's treatment journey, I knew many friends from different cities in the world who helped us and stood with us, including my dear Jeannie, who did not leave me for a day and was the biggest supporter and encourager for me to return to university and I was able to do that in the year 2021. I finished another year and a half of university, with about two semesters and a few hours remaining. I went through some other difficult circumstances that stopped my studies for a while, including my suffering in my life and many problems. I decided to return and continue studying despite that, but unfortunately the war on Gaza began and all was stopped.

All my dreams again, which seem to remain parked until the last hope, stopped. My life is not rosy, but full of suffering and an attempt to remain strong to continue. Reaching is not a simple and easy matter, but rather a road full of stumbles and repeated falls to stand up and try again, and so I cannot stay on the ground, but rather continue to stand after every time I fall into it.

Note: the following formats are used throughout the text to differentiate between message sources.

Text message from Amira

Text message from Jeannie

Media from Amira

Media from Jeannie

All chapter epigraphs are taken from Amira's writings.

PART 1

CHAPTER 1
THE INVASION BEGINS

We are all in God's care, despite the time zone.

Fri, Oct 06 11:30 PM[1]

On October 6, 6:35 a.m., Amira sent me four audio files in succession. They contained nothing but the continuous sounds of gunfire; streaking, falling, exploding missiles; spoken and shouted Arabic; and her terrified, labored breathing as she recorded the beginning of the incursion by Hamas into Israel. However, neither she nor I knew what was happening. Both of us thought it was yet another attack by Israel on Gaza.

Audio of bombs flying overhead, followed by explosions. People begin yelling loudly as they respond to the bombing, followed by loud whistling sounds, then five successive explosions. 0:31

Loud whistling sounds, whooshing sounds, staccato gunfire, then a bomb exploding. People are calling fearfully throughout. 0:18

An explosion—a baby begins crying. Someone calls "ta ally," meaning "come" in Arabic. Voices continue over the sound of the explosion's echo. 0:11

Audio of overhead aircraft, three explosions, and Amira's terrified, labored breath. 0:08

---

1 All times are recorded in Eastern Standard Time.

Sat, Oct 07 12:31 AM

Video of the plume from the first bomb explosions, set against an orange sunrise just beyond the apartment buildings of Amira's neighborhood.

Photo 1A.[2]

Video of explosions. The sun has risen slightly; the sky is beginning to turn blue as more explosions bloom against the sunrise. A rooster is crowing.

Video of the explosions continues. A loud, high-pitched sound seems to streak close by. Bombs continue to explode not too far away.

03:02 AM

They come at sunrise.

Many events during this morning, including the great and the fear of what will happen next

Now you are waiting

The Palestinian resistance dealt a big blow to the occupation and captured many soldiers and stormed the border, and I don't think they will be silent about that

You are right. They won't. I am reading that they fired 5000 rockets in 20 minutes. I didn't read that they have captives.

Still reading.

Yes, and many of the dead in the ranks of the occupation, and the theft of their weapons and equipment, and the kidnapping of some

We know because we've seen the pictures, bring them here

I'm looking for this. Only seeing that one woman was killed.

Their news is so false, dozens have been killed

Look: these resistance fighters after the battle brought the

---

2 Numbered photos appear at the end of their respective chapters.

bodies of dead soldiers, captured Israelis

And these scenes from there dead by the dozen

Photo of four bodies.

This is in Israel?

Yes

Be careful Amira. Silly words as I write them. How do you be careful?

Photo of Israeli woman with her two small red-headed sons.

Bring them prisoners

To Gaza

Don't worry, only what God wants will happen

What is this photo

She is an Israeli woman, they brought her and her children with them, but they will keep them

Children.

She may have refused to leave them and brought them with her, nothing is clear at the moment, but if it happens, they are delivered quickly, they have no work with women and children

Who is circulating these photos

He is a Palestinian journalist from Gaza

God protect them.

09:04 AM

What's happening now

10:36 AM

Explosions and break-ins are still continuing, more than 165 martyrs and 1000 injured

Amira, please send me messages to tell me how you are.

Well, don't worry, my family and I are fine, we stay at home, follow the news

Still, message me.

OK

Thank you.

07:29 PM

Audio of bombs imploding. 0:07

Audio of missiles streaking through the air in rapid succession. 0:08

Audio of muffled bomb explosions followed by people calling out, then more missiles streaking through the air. 0:21

07:59 PM

They sound very close to you

Yes, it's close to the area, everything is close in Gaza, they sent threats to evacuate houses, but where there is no safe place in Gaza, we stay, so we stay at home, nothing to do

I'm sorry Amira. I'm sorry for humanity.

It's okay, we're used to it and we'll try to survive

Used to it. How is one ever used to it. I try to understand.

It happens from time to time, it's terrifying and scary, but there's nothing you can do but try to stay safe and survive, the calm can't continue, we become strong, we get used to the little ones feeling strong, and if we're full of fear inside, we're forced to do it to get over

I am thinking about you. And your strength.

We get it from what we live and go through and from the days the experiences are enough to make us strong

Yes.

Looking for a home

What??

Sun, Oct 08 03:59 AM

We are looking for an apartment outside our city to stay in, as the situation has become very difficult and they have sent threats of eviction

We meaning you and Osama?

No, it's not just Osama and me, it's just the Family, Mom, Dad and my brothers, we're not leaving them

Ok. I thought so. How many of you?

Approximately 10

Where are you now

Still at home

We are waiting to find a place and then head to it, but I didn't find

Please let me know.

I want to know where you are.

OK I will

I got a call

Yes. Of course.

Let me know where you are.

It was a call from the Defense Army Calls for evacuation and gives warning

Because you are close to the Border

Yes

Audio of the call from Israeli Offensive Forces calling for

evacuation.

This is Hamas telling you to evacuate

No, this is the Israel Defense Forces

Oh my God. What are they saying

They are telling you to evacuate?

أجل

Yes

Oh no.

He says to the residents of Beit Hanoun: Operations of the Hamas terrorist organization. The IDF forces are pushing to work against them in their places of residence for your order and safety you must evacuate your homes immediately and go to known shelters the IDF is not interested in harming you and your family members everyone who is near Hamas saboteurs or its centers or sites will endanger his life the house used by terrorist organizations for his military purposes will be targeted Israel Defense Forces

This is the text of the call

You and all your neighbors must go. Can you go to a mosque or a church

I'm sorry. I understand you need to get to safety. I understand you don't know where to go.

Mosques are unsafe, they are being blown up, most of the neighbors have come out to UNRWA centers, schools

But friends are looking for a place and I hope they find

Can you go there?

Mom Refuses it

Ok.

Want to go to that apartment though I'm looking for another

I told her, let them go, and I won't leave my place, but there I won't go

I understand.

How would you travel. Is there a car.

Yes, cars can still move, Osama's friend has one

10 cannot fit.

On two occasions or trying to find another car

05:29 AM

Amira, I can only help you in spirit. I am with you. I want you to stay in contact. If I learn of anything I will contact you.

Well, it's Okay, I'll tell you about it first

01:38 PM

Amira, how are you

I'm OK

Ok. Where are you

At home

Ok.

With all the family?

It's a little quiet now

Ok.

No they go

Who is with you

Photo 1A

CHAPTER 2
LIKE SOMEONE WAITING FOR DEATH

How long are you oh night, and how far are you oh morning?

Sun, Oct 08 01:43 PM

Sunday-the 8th of October-at 8 pm-Beit Hanoun City

Like someone waiting for the near death, I sat in the center of the house listening to those explosions nearby everywhere and the very clear sound of airplanes with the emptiness of the city and empty of its inhabitants, as if it had turned into a ghost town with no souls in it, scary, uninhabited even by the sound of animals and birds, filled with smoke and the smell of gunpowder spreading. The blows were getting closer and closer, and their sound was louder, as if they were hitting the city in succession, in order from place to place. Everyone went chanting "Oh, the spirit beyond you, there is no soul after you". They are clinging to life and trying to escape death. They fled in cars and vehicles, and some of them went out walking for long distances, but Osama and I stayed at home. We hear the sound of explosions, which is almost next to us. Silently there is still some safety with the outbreak of daylight, the fear is when the night closes its tents and the prayers and tours of horror begin, which steal sleep from our eyes and frighten our hearts, the night means "no electricity, no water, no internet," even everything stops at night cata-strophically we do not know the subtleties of the moment and the other, if we were delivered and it was a new day, wel-come that morning, and that our travels, we would meet Allah and forgive us, we witness that there is no god, except Allah and Muhammad is his servant and Messenger

Amira Alzaneen

I was writing

Amira, I sent your writing to my children and 3 of my friends.

Oh good thanks

Yes.

02:20 PM

I am sending it to others. I want your words read. Because you are amazing.

Mon, Oct 09 03:03 AM

Audio of bombs imploding, glass breaking, debris falling. 0:17

Audio of two bombs landing and the resulting echoes, 0:14

Audio of a bomb landing close, debris falling, whispering in Arabic. A cat meows; we hear Amira's fearful breathing. 0:16

Audio of continued bombing, cat meowing, whispers, and heavy, fearful breathing. 0:12

More whispers and breathing. Another bomb drops; debris falls, followed by long whooshing sounds. 0:17

Bomb explosion, glass breaking, a man saying ooohhh. Then what sounds like prayers as debris falls loudly, as if it's in the same room. 0:20

Echoes of bombs. Amira gives a brief utterance with heavy breath. Another explosion; a man's voice, reassuring. 0:11

03:57 AM

Amira answer me

Are you there

04:31 AM

Please tell me you are there

CHAPTER 3
A NIGHT IN HELL

We survived death
We are alive and the dream remains

Mon, Oct 09 07:08 AM

A Night in Hell

Monday - October 9th - 2:30 am - Beit Hanoun City - Al-Qarman Street

The least I can describe that night is that it was a night in hell, and from the heart of death we escaped, thanks to God, from certain death that had besieged us in that house, which was destroyed by the severity of the close strikes and explosions, and most of it fell and its foundations were shaken. The attacks from the occupation planes began at exactly two-thirty and continued, without stopping until six o'clock. I had decided to take a nap until the first explosion occurred next to the house, accompanied by a loud sound of falling glass, thick dust, and the deadly smell of gunpowder. We moved from the basement to the second floor for us to stay in, and from then on, one blow followed another, more severe than the previous one, and fragments, stones, and dust were flying in the air at us, and we could not breathe. The air never stopped. We were reciting the Shahada and praying when we heard the sound of a 16-thousand plane that had returned to where it was. Each time it returned with a harder strike than the one before. The light came, then the sound, then the terrifying explosion. We hugged our heads like children. We chose a corner to take shelter from the strikes. All the glass in the house shattered and the doors were ripped out. And how heavy those hours were, refusing to pass. Complete silence in the place. The area had been completely abandoned. We were certain that our moment was near. Death was everywhere then, and explosions were coming from every direction around the house. It was pitch black. There was no source of light, no communication, or the Internet. We surrendered to our situation and our fate, as it was... It is difficult for anyone to be present to pull you out of the clutches of death in which we are stuck. We decided to try to protect ourselves to the best of our ability and to distance ourselves from anything that might pose a danger and to cling to life until the morning comes. Our tongues are agitated with supplication, the Qur'an, and watching. We turned off our phones. The attack was very fierce. It lasted for hours, and the morning did not come, nor sleep. The smoke was the effect of the explosions. Clouds in the sky. There was no place left around the house that had not been bombed, and the remains collapsed over our heads. We surrendered our affairs to God, and we hardly remember how many strikes were near and far. Morning came and we breathed a little. "The day is hot." The smoke had not yet cleared, and we did not move from our place. We had taken shelter in the sofa seats in front of us. The explosions diminished. The planes moved away, but getting out was still impossible and frightening. The clock moved and it became six-thirty. The glow of the light increased to see the shocking landmarks from afar. Great destruction everywhere. We waited until it became seven. We stood up and from the horror of the shock we froze in our places. There is no intact building, no good house, no store in the same condition. The entire street has had its features removed. Completely with rubble everywhere, and some of the damaged houses were on fire. We had not decided to leave yet. We were inspecting the surroundings. There was no one but us in the place. We were inspecting the massive destruction left by the explosions right next to us. Death was not far away, even meters away, until I inspected my family's home, which had no part in it that had not been destroyed. Everything was taken off. From his place, it was seven-thirty in the morning. There was the sound of people running in the street and shouting, "Go out, come out." We went out carrying our souls on our hands and were defeated by what we saw. There was no street, no houses, no place. The entire area was blown up. How did we survive? How did that night go? We started running quickly for fear of any sudden strike. We ran over rubble, debris, and glass. We walked a lot, and I don't know how I was able to photograph these scenes. We moved away from the danger zone. Praise be to God. He has written a new life for us. A day passed that we thought would not pass and the morning would not come. We left the entire city. We walked long distances to reach a safe place. That day has passed, but this feeling and what we felt. We lived it, it will not go away, and it will not end, and life has a rest.

Amira Alzaneen

Video of her destroyed home and neighborhood. 2:12

Video walking into her destroyed kitchen—the crunching sound of walking on debris and broken glass. 0:06

Video of bathroom with tile and concrete blown out of walls. 0:07

Video of living room with all windows blown out. Some walls missing; floor covered in debris. 0:11

Video of a bedroom, windows gone, debris everywhere, bed still neatly made.

Photo 3A.

Your house

Yes, and the surrounding area

You survived. I cried not knowing your fate Thank God you are alive

No one knows his fate now, we survived that terrible night

Video as Amira walks out of her house, revealing the court-yard covered by a mass of rubble and the destroyed buildings beyond. 0:10

Photos 3B and 3C.

Yes

I hear more planes

Yeah, she didn't stop

Video of Amira walking room to room showing the devastation. Loud crunching as she walks over fallen glass. Not a single room remains inhabitable. 0:51

Amira. I heard the glass breaking in the audios you sent. I knew you were in danger. I heard the fear in your breath. You are alive.

I didn't know. I was waiting.

Yes, alive, we saw death and lived it yesterday, a new life was written for us

For you and Osama. Do you have word from your family

I don't know why Osama separated from them, he left me in an empty house and went, but my family went to that apartment

Osama stayed with you

Didn't Osama stay with you?

I don't know, I'm mad at mom a lot

But Osama with you?

No 😭 😭 😭

You were alone??

No, in an empty house here is his wife, his children, my aunt and her family

Are you all alive

Yes

Thank God.

12:34 PM

Photo 3D: bombed neighborhood, air thick with smoke. Caption reads, "The atmosphere and sky are the effects of explosions."

01:06 PM

Hard to breathe

A lot

05:02 PM

My clothes since yesterday were filled with mud and dust and there is no water I could not take a good shower as I could not bring anything with me

06:37 PM

This is so hard. To not feel clean. Is there bottled water?

Tue, Oct 10 01:14 AM

Yes, the sweetener

04:47 AM

Video from the balcony of the (still intact) neighborhood they fled to. Bombs can be heard as the video searches the beautiful blue sky that still stands against the horizon. 0:19

Same scene as above, but now a gray plume of smoke rises in the distance from the bomb that just landed. 0:18

Same as above; voices can be heard, along with street and

traffic sounds. The gray plume rises higher, seeming to merge with clouds—then the noise of another bomb. 0:33

Same balcony scene with sounds of gunfire, and another gray plume emerging from the neighborhoods on the horizon. 0:29

Photos 3E, 3F, and 3G.

05:11 AM

Where are you

An empty house

Photo of Amira looking exhausted, her wet hair barely covered.

I'm fine, I managed to take a shower, they gave me clean clothes, I feel better now

Who did this for you

My uncle's daughters took out the clothes and my uncle filled the water tanks

In a different house

I'm glad Amira. You have lived through many wars.

Not the same house but they managed to store some water at dawn

Yes, but the night I lived at home last night about all the wars and even my whole life

I feel strange, I'm no longer shocked by something, I don't care about the blows of explosions, the news, I'm no longer eager to know something, like someone waiting for his fate

Yes. It shows in your eyes

Three of my fellow journalists were martyred this morning, I know them and I have a relationship with them, I couldn't grieve, and I didn't feel shocked, I got a big chill, maybe this is the feeling of nothing after that night

I'm sorry. Amira, I believe this is a form of shock

Yes

Your system is in a state of enduring more than possible to cope with at one time. It will take time.

This is what it looks like

Yes. A calm sea outside. A hidden raging lion inside

Yes, there is no ability to show what is in you completely cold

I understand. I do.

From my father.

06:05 AM

Yes. He walked in the Nakba in July of 1948 from Lydda to Ramallah. He experienced too much for his 14-year-old self to handle.

Your experience is deep in you. I will always be here.

Photo 3A

Photo 3B

Photo 3C

Photo 3D

Photo 3E

Photo 3F

Photo 3G

CHAPTER 4
IN THE MIDST OF FIRE

Your night is tiring, O Gaza, and your darkness is so heavy that time makes us hate the night and the darkness of the sky.

Tue, Oct 10 06:08 AM

An Indescribable Feeling in the Midst of Fire

It's like a shock that ran through my veins. I don't know what happened to me at all. The sound of explosions no longer terrifies me. I can't be sad or cry. Likewise, the news, while it's heartbreaking and shocking, I meet it with cold, calm responses until I no longer want to browse or watch it. I'm not aware of anything around me. All of this after that night was as if a part of me died in it, or I was stuck there among the rubble, in that corner in which I was hiding and taking refuge. I was stuck there and I was unable to get out. Everything that is happening is catastrophic, and all of Gaza is under the crosshairs of strikes. There is nothing we do, nothing we change. We wait for the moments to pass quickly, and oh, the day is easier than the night. There are no basics for life and nothing. No Landmarks of this city. Even if the sky is saturated with smoke and gunpowder, how will the rest of the days pass? No one knows. Fear and anxiety no longer come from me, but rather are reflected from those around me. There is no safe spot. Only what is destined for you will happen to you wherever you go. But honestly, I hope it will pass quickly.

Tuesday – October 10th – Gaza – Palestine

Thank you for writing amidst all of this.

This is the most I can do

Thank you for doing it

07:02 AM

The siege is a terrible thing, there is no electricity, no water, no food, no internet, everything must be secured, shopping and storage, as it looks like it will take a long time, I don't know how, but this is what needs to be thought about, providing supplies for difficult moments

Yes. I saw Israeli officials talking about it. Monsters.

Too much, no matter what they have, they try to squeeze in every way

Yes. And pretend self defense

Yes, that's what's happening

Video from same balcony, with two gray plumes of smoke rising above not-too-distant buildings. Sound of bombs dropping.

Two more explosions as the camera searches the horizon, mixed with the common daily sounds of traffic and horns honking.

But they suffered a big loss in the financial markets due to the high exchange rate of the dollar against the shekel, which reached 395 shekels per 100$

Yes, makes sense.

Yes

Israel is still dropping bombs?

Yes, everywhere

Still casualties?

Less than yesterday Now there are 5 injuries

Ok.

01:55 PM

Video from the same balcony as above, but at night. An eerie orange flash, an orange plume, then blackness interrupted by scatterings of city lights. Then the sound of a bomb dropping.

Photo 4A.

Wed, Oct 11 05:00 AM

You know Mustafa Ali as well as Mustafa the captain was my colleague at the university, my friend, his wife, his child, as well as his sister and his family all went victims at dawn today after their house was blown up over their heads without warning

08:03 AM

Oh God. I'm sorry. I'm sorry Amira.

09:36 AM

Video from the same balcony, massive plumes of smoke rising from what looks like only a few blocks away. Quick sound of another explosion.

Photo 4B.

Where are you? Who are you with?

My sister Warda, her husband and her son went to UNRWA schools and asked me for money to buy diapers and food for them, and then I found out that I lost my wallet in the bombing that day at home

Oh no.

But you are with them?

There is no problem with my official papers in my possession and we do not know what happened in the house where the area was blown up again yesterday evening

Neither my sister and her husband were with my mother in the apartment and left her because of the bad situation and went to school with her husband's parents

Is your mother ok?

They're all fine, but she's struggling and praying for me. She hates me so much

She

She doesn't hate you.

She doesn't do it because I didn't carry out her plan and go there, she talks bad about me

She puts her fear on you of her own life.

She knows your strength.

She has it too.

I'll help you however I can.

Very tired these days

 You have lived 5 lifetimes And this is the most difficult

Yes.

05:00 PM

I'm going to bed, I'm tired of thinking how to save everything, things are complicated, I'm trying to sleep

You must sleep. It is your job now to sleep and gain your strength. I have shared your words with many. My son posted your video on Instagram. You are helping.

This makes me happy and I hope that the truth will reach the whole world and I will have made a difference

Yes.

I will keep sharing.

Wed, Oct 11 05:13 PM

I explain to you how the sound as it descends pulls your whole body to the ground with a feeling of magnets to get under and the explosion between shaking your body like electricity is quiet if you hear safely, I promised what I heard to be a martyr and after what your body shakes with palpitations, heart beats, some and some, and it aches and tingles this is the case with us in Gaza these days, and on the Dark, Black Nights, our tongues are repeating prayers, testimony and remembrance all the time without stopping.

Your calls to us all the time 💔

Amira Alzaneen

Photo 4A

Photo 4B

CHAPTER 5
THE FLEEING BEGINS

Our last wish is not to be anonymous corpses

Thu, Oct 12 04:56 PM

Where are you?

My place

Ok.

06:26 PM

Thanks. I am thinking about you

Fri, Oct 13 12:55 AM

The situation is very bad, the explosions are increasing, the citizens are leaving, we don't know what to do and where to go, the situation is catastrophic

02:56 AM

I'm very bad I lost all my money 300$

I had stashed them for any emergency and today since we are going out again and I will give my sister and bring some needs, I checked them in place and did not find them

08:08 AM

Video of moving traffic, some cars with multiple people sitting on the hoods. People riding in wagons filled with their possessions, pulled by donkeys. People on foot. All fleeing south.

Photo 5A.

11:30 AM

How can you receive money?

Sat, Oct 14 01:19 AM

Amira are you there

02:16 AM

Are you there

02:20 PM

Good evening Jeannie, how are you? I just want to tell you I'm ok. I'm now with my uncle's family in Shifa hospital, staying for two days. No internet here, I just today have a little internet to send a message to friends to tell them that I'm ok

The views here are unbearable, I hope the days will pass quickly

Remittance offices are open during certain hours of the day in the daytime on some days

Are you able to get to Gaza City to the Greek Orthodox Church

To be honest with you there is nowhere safe in Gaza. Now we still in Shifa hospital, the most safe place here.

But if something happens, we will try to go to the south, but they are liars, they strike there too

I know. HOWEVER I do not think they will bomb the church. You must do what you feel is best. There are 400! people there. I cried all morning wondering where you were. Thank you for telling me. I feel you are like a daughter to me.

I know that the church may be a place that's safe in Gaza, but a few minutes that day they bomb it and ask about that. They say that the bombing....there

I hope we can find a safe place, but there is no place in Gaza, we will try and I will try to stay in constant contact with you, your prayers always

Audio: "I will send for you a story that happened yesterday for us in Shifa hospital. It was very sad, very bad, but we are okay."

Photo 5A

CHAPTER 6
AL-SHIFA HOSPITAL

Nothing to say. Silence in throats.
The scenes are catastrophic and indescribable.

Sat, Oct 14 02:39 PM

Friday Evening and Saturday Dawn, the 13th and 14th of October - Al-Shifa Hospital - Gaza - the Seventh Day in a Row

After the many threats from the occupation to evacuate homes and move from northern to southern Gaza, they were threats since the early morning hours of Friday, but we did not care about them because we absolutely refuse to leave our homes. The scenes of people moving in large gatherings are almost no different from those that occurred in the 1948 migration as our day passed. It happened until six o'clock on Friday evening, and the occupation planes targeted a house behind the place where we live, or rather, we took refuge in it after the destruction of our houses, which was empty. The house was struck above its occupants without warning, and the strike was followed by four more that made the walls of the house shake violently. We decided at that time that the house must be evacuated, as we were on the fifth floor, we were four families instead of a family, and the number exceeded 30 people, including women, men, youth, and children. We thought of spending that night in the basement of the building, which all its residents had vacated earlier in the same day. After much thought, we decided to leave for fear of the building being blown up and collapsing. We remained stuck in that place and there was a lack of oxygen, as they repeatedly warned of intensifying strikes for that day, so we moved from our place, unaware of our destination. We walked a lot with thousands of people in the street, similar to our situation, for distances that I can hardly remember. We searched for a means of transportation, but to no avail. We thought, should we go to shelter centers or not? The south or the hospital. There was no certain place, as the threat included evacuating everything in the north and Gaza area. In the end, we chose to go to Al-Shifa or Baptist Hospital and stay there until the morning came. With great difficulty, we found a small bus that could accommodate a number not exceeding 10 people. I do not know how we were able to sit. We were in it even though the women were the ones who stayed in it and the men continued to walk behind us, except for the children. We moved a little, and there was a bombing nearby, which led to my uncle, who stayed with us, being injured in some way in the head. The fall made us all sad, and we ran and screamed like crazy people in the street towards him. We arrived and his head was dead. He bled a lot, the wound was large and not simple, and we tried to find a car to take him to Al-Shifa Hospital, until he went first, and we followed him on the bus quickly, praying to God not to cause us grief. We arrived at the hospital unaware, and quickly headed towards the emergency room, which was filled with the smell of blood everywhere-. We searched for him until we found him, and we followed what was happening with trembling hearts. He was transferred for a CT scan, which took a long time due to the large number of injured people waiting in front of the radiology room for their turn to come. It ended and we waited near the door. It was decided to admit him for operations urgently. We went from the emergency department to the building in which the operating department was located. His head did not stop bleeding and we could not move because the hospital was crowded with people. We could not. We all went up, but those who went informed us that the operation would require 3 hours of time, and that would be after his turn came due to the large number. As you know, we had found a corner in the hospital where we sat on the floor, waiting and praying for him. We consoled, supported, and strengthened each other a little. Hours passed and the operation ended, and he remained under observation. We couldn't see him, so we went looking for another place to sit because of the extreme cold of the weather. We walked a little.

Hundreds of thousands spread out on the ground and cover the sky in every corner of the hospital and its courtyard, all of them fleeing from the terrifying bombing in the Gaza Strip. We walked with great caution because of the darkness and for fear of stepping on someone who fell asleep after long hours of fatigue and exhaustion and to no avail. There was no place. We returned to where we were sitting on the floor. It is al most 2 o'clock on Saturday morning, and the number of people sleeping has doubled. They are waiting for the morning to come with great fear, and their eyes have not tasted sleep. They move here and there. There is no internet in the place. We are cut off from the world. We do not know what is happening outside. We hear the sound of explosions and planes that are getting closer and closer, and we do not know its location and the sound of ambulances that are arriving. It goes laden with martyrs and wounded. Hardly one comes out. Another comes for hours full of exhaustion. We pray and pray and pray to God that this calamity does not continue, as the situation is catastrophic, and the tragedy is very great. Destruction, losses, victims and massacres are countless in just one week. Gaza is bleeding with pain from every corner of it. There is not a house that has not been visited. Death, sadness, and pain, and no one feels our condition, and the genocide to which we are exposed, and the great destruction of the country. We cried out to the whole world, and there was no answer. We waited for the sunrise to reassure ourselves of my uncle's condition and to decide where we would go and how the days would pass. We thought a lot and there was no answer?? Will we survive or will we be among those who left??? I don't know, there are no words that can help me to describe this amount of events. No mind can comprehend and no one believes how we survive every day from what we live. We fear death without recognizable features or without funerals that anyone knows about. Here is Gaza, whose skies are filled with gunpowder and all its suburbs are visited by death.

Will there be more chapters of what happens??? Amira Alzaneen

Gaza - Palestine

I'm telling you about the situation in this hospital, in this place.

The only thing I can do at this moment and this day, at this place is writing. Staying without internet is a very bad thing and all the time I was writing what's happening, what I can tell the world, what I can tell everyone what happened here.

04:10 PM

And you will.

Sun, Oct 15 04:10 AM

My uncle is gone, he's dead

07:00 AM

I'm sorry. I'm sorry.

12:44 PM

💔 💔 💔

Tue, Oct 17 07:39 PM

Amira are you there

Wed, Oct 18 03:10 AM

Hi how are you I'm still OK

04:02 AM

The hospital and the church were destroyed. did you see the massacre

05:41 AM

Yes. I did.

Where we go

Where are you now

In the same place the patient's zone in the kindergarten with difficulty we get the internet and charge for the phone

Yes. I knew you had to find a place. Are you with your Aunt?

Yes

I am thinking about you all the time. My prayers are with Gaza and with you.

I hope that what is happening does not continue and ends as soon as possible

The whole world is with you now. People are rising up all over the world. Israel has been caught in a big lie.

We wish that, we felt so much that we were alone

They claimed Hamas bombed the hospital. But the world knows they are lying.

08:15 AM

Yes

We're going to get out of here, we don't know where to go

Thu, Oct 19 05:36 AM

The scenes of the last hours in the Gaza Strip, so that you will be able to follow, consist in the burial of bodies and burying them in cemeteries other than their places of residence, as well as inspecting the wounded and inspecting the remains of the victims, as well as the recovery of those whose bodies remained under the rubble and the targeted houses, and the most case is the crowd inside the shelter centers related to UNRWA schools, and the situation there is deplorable and a very crying state. Families who have lost their children, lost their loved ones, lost their property and homes and cannot return because of fear and shelling. Here is Gaza and the coverage continues

Fri, Oct 20 06:15 AM

How Are you

07:23 AM

Hey. I'm here. Where are you

Well, in an empty house we stayed

Ok. Keep talking to me. You are with your Aunt?

Yes

17 people

I'm glad you are with people. Are you eating

08:18 AM

Yeah, we're trying to save, it's hard, but we're trying 🙏

09:28 AM

Hi how are you

#Imagining

Can you imagine waking up at 5 in the morning just to be among the first 50 in line for bread?

Can you imagine walking over 6 kilometers to fill a jug with either sweet or salty water, knowing it won't make much of a difference?

Can you imagine having to go to someone with a solar panel to ask, "Could you please charge my phone for half an hour?" and in return, they get only 20% charge, and you have to use your phone with maximum power saving just to make it through the day?

Can you imagine going to the supermarket, wandering around and craving a dish, but in the end, you only buy a block of cheese because you don't even have gas to cook?

Can you imagine that by 7 in the evening, you start interacting with people? Can you imagine living up to this moment?

Can you imagine that what you're living is reality, not fiction? Yes, by God...

• Cut. - Take the House.

• OK, we sent you cans of hummus and mortadella!

• My little brother is dead.

• OK, we sent you bread!

• And mom's dead.

• OK, we sent you tuna and sardines!

• Even my father died.

• God bless him! We have sent you wine and milk!

• Understand, stupid! All my family is dead!

• OK, we have sent you several full suffices for each family! Don't Worry!!

12:10 PM

I am posting all of this on Facebook

12:58 PM

CHAPTER 7
ST. PORPHYRIUS GREEK ORTHODOX CHURCH

My friends list has become a graveyard 💔

Sun, Oct 22 03:29 PM

Sorry for the loss of your relatives

04:29 PM

How did you know?

From media

Mon, Oct 23 10:26 AM

Ok. Yes. Thank you. I think all the losses are horrendous. So grateful to hear from you.

I didn't know because of the power outage and the lack of internet, I saw one named Viola and her sister from the Amash family, so I knew they were from your family

My condolences to you and my heart is very sad, I hope this will end soon

We all hope so. If you can go to the church, we think we are able to get funds to friends still there. They survived. My daughter raised funds and they were sent yesterday.

12:29 PM

I don't know in which church they are now if you can communicate with them and try to go when you are sure

Greek Orthodox Church.

Church of St. Porphyrius in Gaza City. This is the same church.

But haven't they been destroyed

12:57 PM

No. One wall collapsed. Where women and children were sleeping.

That's why the victims were women and children

Yes

They will receive funds soon. Tell me if you go.

Well, I'll tell you that if they agree, we should leave the house and go somewhere else, there is no safe place in Gaza, it's scary

01:20 PM

Yes. You may at least find food there.

Yes

I'll try

I understand. Be careful.

Tue, Oct 24 02:34 AM

Good morning, I want to ask, Should I stay at the church to get food and supplies, or can I just go there and return some to those with me, since we are 18 people, me, an empty house, my aunt and others?

03:00 AM

I am going to ask someone. Yes, it is difficult because there are so many. I will ask someone to prepare some supplies for you. I don't know what they have right now, or what is even available. Do you have running water? Do you have any way of cooking? I'm sorry to ask

09:45 AM

There is clean water, but we are trying to save gas for cooking, we are trying to save as much as we can

I apologize for the delay the phone was in the charger and no internet

Wed, Oct 25 05:24 AM

I hope you can get there and get help. I am thinking about you every day Amira.

06:15 AM

They talked to me and they'll follow up

Ok good. Are you close to where they are

The place they told me about is far away, but not much can be reached inside Gaza, and the market is also close to see what will happen

I hope you can reach them. I am told last night was a terrible night.

Yes, it was a difficult night everywhere in Gaza, the beating is crazy everywhere, the ambulances and the smell of gunpowder

We would have passed and we are still fine, thank God

Thank God.

06:43 AM

Thu, Oct 26 08:23 AM

How are you today we are fine and we are trying to stay so

I am thinking about you! Sending love.

As usual, I have no energy left to write, so I don't know what's going on outside. things are getting worse

You are surviving a war. How to write? If you do, I am sharing everything. Do you know where your parents, brothers and sisters are?

Yes, we are fighting to survive and stay well and these days go by

They are with you now?

My family in the south, in Rafah, don't communicate with us, they're angry, it's not important, they're just fine

Oh God. Ok.

I know their news from my cousins when they only communicate with them

I love you Amira.

And I also love you very much

We will see each other again.

CHAPTER 8
QUESTIONS

All roads lead to death in Gaza
Rest in peace all of you

"We try, as much as we can, with the energy we have left, to stay well and fight to survive and stay alive. Even though every corner of this place is tinged with death, all that's left in us has faded away. No time to cry, no time to be shocked, no time for us to live as we used to. Everything has turned upside down. We no longer know the days and dates; they all blend together. Daily tasks have become identical - getting some water, charging phones, waiting in line for bread and gas, securing whatever is necessary. And of course, it won't be enough before six in the evening. The streets are empty of everything, eerie and still. Night comes with its loneliness, and prayers and supplications pass the heavy time. A new day arrives, and we are still alive, for some time. We turn to the internet to reassure and reply, 'We're still alive,' so as not to be counted among the missing. Browsing the news quickly pains the heart, just to know what's happening. These days of ours are alike, with nothing different except the numbers of the missing and the destruction. Will we overcome? Will we stay? Will this end? Who will remain to tell what happened? Amira Alzaneen, 26/10/2023. The city that fights to stay alive, Gaza."

We will see each other again. I hope

Thinking of you today Amira

Okay, no internet, no electricity

I understand. But now I know you are there.

"Not all the missing are dead, but all the living in Gaza are missing in one way or another.

All of us, our limbs severed into parts scattered everywhere. One body, all its feelings and emotions, dispersed and fragmented, absent, fearful, lost, confused, a mind filled with endless questions without any answers. We are scattered everywhere.

Where will we go? When will our turn come? What comes next? Will everything pass?

Missing without communication, fear, horror, loss, shocks, loved ones, and understanding what happened will take decades, and perhaps we will remain stuck in the center of what happened. The dead have been buried and are now safely underground, their souls in the care of the Merciful. As for us, the living, this world with its commodities has buried us, and we are still above trying to understand, in vain. Will we really survive? Or will the rest of our lives be filled with sadness and grief?

If we go and become part of the earth and under the soil, know that we loved life with all that is in us, and we approached war only out of compulsion, and God chose for us what is best and grand for us. And if we remain among the living and above the earth, we will narrate what we lived through for everyone in the world to hear. We will be among those who snatched life from the jaws of death and shattered the bottle in which we were trapped. Our time for farewell has not come, but rather, it is time to meet again when God wills."

- Amira Alzaneen, 27/10/2023

Brilliant. Thank you.

I am posting everything you write.

I appreciate it and I am glad that many people are getting what we are living and going through and they know lies

Yes. I will look into creating a book from this by you. Keep writing. I am listening.

I will try to write down everything that comes to mind, so everything will remain stuck in my head, all the moments and what I experienced

Yes. It is important. You are speaking to the world. I will make sure of it. 💚👥

You ARE speaking to the world 🌎

And I hope that the facts will reach this world and stop what is happening

11:51 AM

Audio of continuous gunfire, low sounds of people speaking. 0:24

Video—bright flashes of orange as bombs explode, then darkness. Another flash, darkness, continuous gunfire. People calling. Distant rumble of exploding bombs and debris falling. 0:11

Continued video—one orange flash in the darkness, drones overhead, gunfire. A bomb explodes, a baby babbles. 0:13

Multiple flashes of orange in the darkness. Women talking. Gunfire continues. Children's voices; a couple of explosions; women and men talking. Drones overhead. 0:29

Loud pop/crack with another orange flash. Three rounds of gunfire. Explosion. Drones overhead; people talking. 0:16

Women's voices; someone utters a tsk-tsk. Orange flash, rounds of gunfire, drones. A man's voice. 0:10

Darkness with black plumes visible. Rapid gunfire. Women, men, and children's voices. 0:15

Several bright-orange flashes, more rapid gunfire. A bomb reverberates. Drones; people talking, including children. 0:45

People continue talking. More orange flashes in the darkness. Bombs continue to drop; gunfire and drones. 0:27

Photos 8A , 8B.

Photo 8A

Photo 8B

CHAPTER 9
AMIDST THE BLAZE OF FIRE

I wonder if it will happen tomorrow

Fri, Oct 27 04:18 PM

Gaza Amidst the Blaze of Fire from North to South:

On the twenty-seventh of October, at exactly seven in the evening, a catastrophe occurred in Gaza. The darkened sky of the city turned into a terrifying day due to the blazing fireballs that swept through it from north to south. They were followed by a series of explosions that didn't cease for a moment, surpassing twenty within less than a minute.

Every corner of Gaza was engulfed in flames, and night turned into day in a horrifying night where you could disappear from your sight at any moment. The air was filled with catastrophic terror and insane explosions. Communication networks were cut off, and electricity supplies were severed, intensifying the darkness with the smoke and powder that covered the sky of the region with its thick blanket.

Screams filled the air everywhere, and pleas for help were made to the civil defense and medical teams that couldn't reach the affected areas due to the collapse of transmission networks.

We sit in the middle of our homes, all of us waiting, looking through the windows at the flicker of flames in the sky, muffling our ears a little to reduce the intensity of the continuous explosions that were getting closer and closer. We console each other that they might have receded and stopped, but they returned worse than before.

Gaza was isolated from the world, with mass massacres and horrifying destruction filling every place. No one knows anything about us, and we know nothing about anyone. Will this night pass? If it does, you will read my words, and if it doesn't, they will remain trapped in my notes.

A night of hell in every sense of the word, a heavy time that neither passed nor ended. A frightening stillness that sends shivers down the spines of humans. We've had enough, we can't bear any more. Our hearts have reached our throats.

We survived once again, but for how long?

Amira Alzaneen – Gaza that is disappearing and dying.

08:42 PM

It's so scary, it's like I'm alone here

09:26 PM

Loneliness is the hardest emotion. The hardest of all. Everything falls away but ourself. I am thinking of you constantly. If only I could tell you how much I care. How brave I think you are.

Sat, Oct 28 02:56 AM

I added to it

Sat, Oct 28 02:57 AM

Gaza Amidst the Blaze of Fire from North to South:

On the twenty-seventh of October, at exactly seven in the evening, a catastrophe occurred in Gaza. The darkened sky of the city turned into a horrifying day due to the flaming projectiles that swept from north to south. It was followed by a series of explosions that didn't cease for a moment, surpassing twenty in less than a minute.

Every corner of Gaza was ablaze, and night turned into a terrifying day, as if you could disappear from sight at any moment. The air was filled with a catastrophic terror and frenzied explosions. Communication networks were cut off, and power supplies were disrupted, intensifying the darkness with the thick cover of smoke and gunpowder that blanketed the region's sky.

Screams filled the air everywhere, and pleas for help echoed for civil defense and medical teams that couldn't reach the affected areas due to the collapse of transmission networks.

We sat in the middle of our homes, all of us anxious, gazing through the windows at the flicker of fire in the sky, muffling our ears a little to lessen the intensity of the successive explosions that drew nearer and nearer. We consoled each other that they might have receded and stopped, but they returned worse than before.

Gaza was isolated from the world, mass atrocities and horrifying destruction filled every space. No one knows anything about us, and we know nothing about anyone. Will this night pass? If it does, you will read my words, and if it doesn't, they will remain trapped in my notes.

We were completely cut off from the world, not just the world, but even within the borders of this isolated city, there isn't even a handful of communication networks or internet. You feel like the solitary inhabitant of this city, we don't know the news, we don't know what happened outside, and where it happened. Movement is completely paralyzed, sound is inaudible, and visibility is impossible, even helpless to check on anyone, life has come to a halt, everything has stopped, we wait for our turn.

A night of hell, in every sense of the word, a heavy time that neither passed nor ended. A frightening stillness that makes human skin crawl. We've had enough, we can't bear it any longer. Our hearts have reached our throats.

We survived once again, We are not okay

But for how long?

Amira Alzaneen - Gaza that fades and dies

08:07 AM

Thank you for telling me you are there

11:07 AM

I'm here

I'm trying to communicate with someone to go to the super-market and get supplies and I can't, no networks

12:16 PM

It is difficult for anyone to answer. Are you close to the church now

12:55 PM

I was thinking in the daytime to go there tomorrow to check on them

Ok. Good luck. Let me know.

Sun, Oct 29 02:50 AM

"I am Amira from Gaza, miraculously connected to the in-ternet. This might be my last post. All internet and commu-nications are cut off in Gaza. We can't reach our families, we don't know what happened to them! We don't know where the bombings are, who is alive and who has passed away, no news about what's happening! But please remember that you left Gaza alone... very much alone."

03:10 AM
Communication networks are back

05:35 AM
Thank you.

I am posting your words. People are sharing.

12:58 PM

Thank you so much for everything, your presence and support today I went and shopped from the store what we need.

I'm talking to you from the hallway of the house, we're all sitting next to each other and the kittens, after there were explosions nearby in the ocean, we can't get out because of the bad situation and the wild night, we're fine until the moment

Photo 9A: five tiny black kittens in a box, with mama cat sitting next to them on a blue blanket.

They are 5 little ones who are afraid wherever I go, I take them with me that we are displaced, I'm afraid these are souls too

Mon, Oct 30 04:20 PM
Where are you today?

Tue, Oct 31 08:35 AM
We spent a bad night in the basement, the beating was severe, we went out at one o'clock in the morning, we walked a lot, arrived at a school accommodation center, where we stayed in the stairwell area

I am checking for you, even in the middle of the night. You are with your group.

There was no internet connection, now I called All right, all 18 people

Crazy artillery was hitting everywhere

Amira, none of us can imagine this pain.

09:31 AM

Do you have the kitties??

11:22 AM

Of course, they were so scared I couldn't leave them. I brought them with me.

You are the best. The most wonderful.

11:38 AM

Like you

Thu, Nov 02 10:32 AM

Where are you

12:03 PM

Here I am trying to write to you, but the internet will not

I just making sure you are there.

CHAPTER 10
AN EVENTFUL DAY

Everything on earth is not enough philosophy
to describe what is happening in Gaza

Fri, Nov 03 02:14 AM

Today was eventful. We accomplished many tasks. We woke up at 6 AM, didn't sleep much due to the intense shelling at night. We headed to the bakery hoping to get some bread, as we haven't had any for three days. Upon arrival, the place was crowded and we left empty-handed. We decided to go north to the house, despite the dangerous situation, but we had no other choice. We needed many things like flour, cooking utensils, and some mattresses for sleeping. We walked about 10 kilometers on foot. The place was quiet and eerie. We reached the fifth floor, gathered the items quickly, and the sound of explosions continued. We took what we could and went back down. We walked again; the streets were empty. We found a means of transportation, a donkey-drawn vehicle. We loaded our belongings and climbed on. We returned to the school where we are sheltering. Everyone was dispersing in some streets. We arrived and didn't get a chance to rest. We decided to clean the place, sort what we brought, and then prepare the dough for baking. There was no other option. We made a fire oven and cooked some food like beans and tomatoes, along with quick snacks. We also filled up on water and searched for a place to charge our phones. The sad part is that after all this, I couldn't find any water in the school to bathe. I've been feeling suffocated for two days in this state, but today passed with everything it contained. I'm very tired but happy that I'm able to get and provide what we might need to continue, even if it's difficult. I wrote this message at 6 AM and couldn't send it due to the lack of internet. I'll send it to you along with some pictures of my eventful day.

02:12 AM

Photos 10A and 10B: Amira on the cart with her possessions.

The donkey pulls the cart and its drivers. We hear bombing in the background. 0:06

Photo 10C.

Photo 10D: an outdoor oven, bread, and cooked tomatoes.

Photo 10E: Amira's hand holding a small plastic cup of coffee,.

Boys kicking around an object in a schoolyard; the half walls surrounding the back are painted in murals. 0:13

Photo 10F.

That's since yesterday

Photo 10A

Photo 10B

Photo 10C

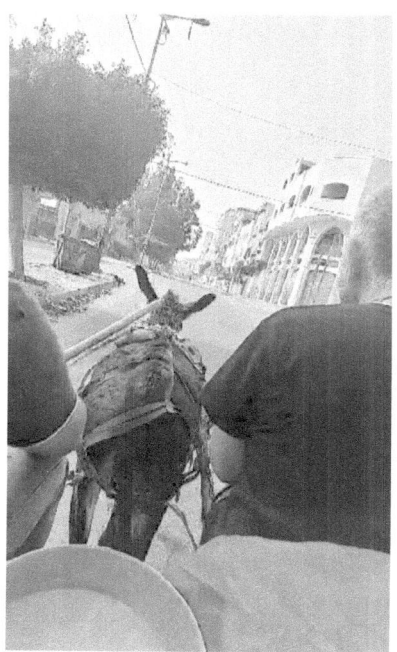

Photo 10D

Photo 10E

Photo 10F

CHAPTER 11
LAND OF THE PHOENIX

How many sad people you see,
nothing but contentment on their faces,
but their hearts are torn apart

Fri, Nov 03 02:48 AM

A text arrived late a whole day because there was no internet.

- 6 O'clock in the Morning from the Land of the Phoenix that Never Dies.

Morning came and so did the daylight, which reassures you a bit because you can move and know what's happening around you, unlike the long night where you isolate yourself from everything except the sound of strikes, fear everywhere, and the looming strike.

Where are we heading? We moved many times because the danger got closer. Our shelter is now a school for refugees called "People and Forgetfulness." We took a class to shelter 19 people, four families, less than two meters apart for each family. We lie on the ground because we left in a hurry without being able to take anything. Oh yes, and we took cloth for "Suka" and her five young ones with us because they are scared, and they are still souls.

At night, men take turns outside, doing our usual morning tasks since sunrise: providing water, bread, organizing, figuring out what today's meal will be, which might not be available in the first place. Charging batteries and phones if possible, but hardly anything is safe. Not the tree, not the stone, not the animal, not the inanimate, neither the human nor the child, not even in the womb of a mother, nor in a hospital or school, no car or vehicle, not even the bakeries are safe.

You're not safe awake or asleep, and you're not in any state or place because there's no peace. It doesn't matter if it's the beginning of the week or the end, or what the date or day is. What matters is that morning comes, and there's still a new day. Yes, everything in us is faded, but as long as we open our eyes, it means we're still alive. Not well, but still here. We check on ourselves because at any moment, we might become just another number added to the list of the missing. A new day, Lord, may it be different. Lord, may there be relief, unlike the days that have passed. Your mercy, Lord.

Not well, but still alive. Amira Alzaneen.

Gaza – 2-11-2023.

By the way, today marks the 106th year since the infamous Balfour Declaration.

Part of the daily tasks after walking about ten kilometers to get flour because we didn't find bread and kitchen supplies to use.

A great achievement despite all the exhaustion. "The smell of land or nothingness."

03:35 AM

I'll send you a video I made

It is good to hear from you. It is good to see you. The streets are quiet. Before, they were bustling, full, noisy. I hear the overhead drone of the invader. I am glad you are with people. Phoenix. Yes. From the ashes you continue to rise.

Please hug all of your friends for and from me.

07:08 AM

The internet will download the video

07:53 AM

I see your pictures. Maybe the video is too long and the video connection is weak

11:34 AM

Here are some excerpts without our photos that I have combined on Palestinian music that I want to publish with the text

Ok!

You are sending more?

I am ready and waiting

No just one

Ok

This with video

Ahh, ok.

11:57 AM

The situation is very bad. They bombed the Al-Shifa Hospital and the Indonesian

The Indonesian?? Last night?

Video compilation of the previous scenes, including baking bread, riding in the donkey art, the coffee in a plastic cup, young boys playing in the schoolyard, and the black kittens, set to sad Palestinian violin music. 0:51

Not today either a little earlier and they say there is a massacre

Oh God. Ok.

Sun, Nov 05 04:49 AM

The world is marching. please message me. Please message me today if you can.

Photo 11A: march in Washington, DC, on November 4, 2023, for Palestine.

04:36 PM

Amira

Mon, Nov 06 03:39 AM

Audio: "Hello, Jeannie. How are you? I am sorry I cannot contact you for the last day—no internet, no charge on my phone. I'm okay. I'm still in the school. Everything is good; we are fine. I wish all of that ends very soon. Thanks for your support, for all supporters in the world; thank you for everything.

"I hope the support of the world and their voice will change something and end this genocide and war."

03:53 AM

Amira, I am so happy to hear this. I woke up and looked at my phone and saw your message. I listened to your message and I am grateful to hear your voice thank you so much. Yes, I know that it is difficult to charge your phone. I understand that, it's ok, you never have to say sorry. Just message me when you can, and I'm glad that you're ok in the school.

Photo 11B: coffee in a real ceramic cup!

04:46 AM

Coffee!!!!

Yes

Tue, Nov 07 02:08 AM

Clean the school

Amira, what happened

Children clean the school in exchange for bringing a football to play with

Ok. I didn't know what you meant!

I sent a video and it hasn't arrived yet

Thinking about you every day.

Video of children sweeping the school playground. 0:10

Photo 11C.

I also think about everything in this world, tomorrow and life

Yes. How it must be. Only you can know. Keep writing. Keep recording into your phone. I am listening. No one else can do it.

I will whenever I can

I know. And I know that sometimes there aren't words

You know, sometimes I want to break down and cry and I can't, and I want to scream and explode and I can't even grieve so much that we have to pull together and stay strong, at least these days

Amira, you are living through the worst nightmare. None of us here can imagine what you endure every moment. Screaming, exploding, one day I hope you will have the safety to express all of this. Many are with you. We are marching in the streets all over the world.

I hope there are still days left to express what we have lived

Yes.

Me too.

09:21 AM

It looks like I'm going to get sick, my body hurts a lot, I can't move, I hope it's not a virus

Oh no. Is there someone with you to help you

Everyone is here but there are no medicines and no cures even in the pharmacy

I know. But you will be ok. Rest. I pray for you today.

10:11 AM

Wed, Nov 08 10:42 AM

I did something today, I went to the supermarket and bought several bags of sweets that are not precious, the price does not exceed 2 shekels, and I distributed them to the children at school, it was a nice feeling and they were very happy. I did not take pictures, my phone was in the charger, but I will try to repeat it

Beautiful.

Thu, Nov 09 05:03 PM

Thinking of you Amira

Photo 11A

Photo 11B

Photo 11C

CHAPTER 12
TO RAFAH

O Allah, I ask you for the best of this day, its opening,
its victory, its light, its blessing, its guidance,
and I seek refuge in you from the evil that is in it.

Fri, Nov 10 02:16 AM

Today is gonna be a long ride

We are moving to south Gaza on foot

With News that we are thinking of going to the South

08:06 AM

Ok. You must go to safest place

Sat, Nov 11 04:31 AM

Good morning from the south of Gaza from the city of Rafah how are you. We arrived here yesterday there was no internet so we did not communicate and my family arrived. I will arrange the writing and send it to you

06:29 AM

Thank you. Amira.

Sun, Nov 12 04:42 AM

The Safe Passage... The Road of Death Friday, November 10, 2023

At 10:30 in the morning we decided to depart and migrate once again, finally, after the intensity of the shelling and the worsening dangerous situation. After we fled from the north to Gaza, we continued the journey from Gaza to its south.

We prepared our belongings and necessities since the early morning hours, lightening the load as much as possible so that the burdens wouldn't weigh us down. The road is long, difficult, and exhausting, and we do not yet know what we will encounter.

We walked a distance of about 5 kilometers on foot from the Daraj area in Gaza to a school. After that, we found a cart pulled by a donkey that transported us from our location to Al Kuwait roundabout, the beginning of the safe passage from Gaza to its south.

The place is crowded with people, and thousands are flocking to move: women, elders, children, the elderly – we encountered all categories on our way.

The march is collective; you raise one hand with the identification card, a bag on your back, and a sack in your hand. Using the mobile phone is prohibited, and you proceed without looking around or making any movement that could cause harm.

The road is full of sand barricades, behind which snipers and tanks hide. A continuous march to confront the occupation, alongside the smell of gunpowder and the tragic scene of destruction. There are scattered bodies in some places, besides that accursed flag rising above our land.

We continued the journey, walking another 10 kilometers among the displaced from the north, Gaza, and different places.

We reached beyond Wadi Gaza, where we ran out of breath,

exhausted from the intense heat and lack of provisions. We stopped at the entrance of Bureij and sat to rest for a while.

Ten minutes passed, and we were surprised by the sound of artillery explosions for a brief moment, and the shrapnel was around us. None of us was touched, thank God, after our party split into two groups – some reached Bureij, and some are still walking the valley road. We survived once again.

Afterward, we headed to the Maghazi camp, sat on the street to rest, ate pickles to ease our hunger, and neighbors brought us water. We waited to find transportation to head south.

We found transportation to Rafah in the form of a half-truck; we all sat in it, passing by people who were still walking, until we reached a safe place. The road is exhausting and long; we reached Rafah, searched a lot for a shelter center for displaced people with an available space, to no avail.

We went beyond the Yibna camp east of Rafah, found a school crowded with refugees, and decided to stay for the day. The women stayed in the classrooms, and the men in the schoolyard, lying on the ground and covering the sky. There are no life essentials here, no services, far away from anything.

We moved to the UNRWA's supply stores, no different from any place with thousands of displaced people. Tents everywhere inside and outside, significant overcrowding but manageable.

There, I reunited with my family after a long separation of more than a month due to this devastating war. Safety is what we are seeking; 70% of the population in the governorates of the sector is concentrated in its south, and their lives revolve around here.

The safe passage is nothing but the road of death with all that it entails, shrouded in the scent of tragedy and death.

Will we surrender?

Is it the last time we depart?

Will we be the ones to tell the story, or will the story be told about us?

Amira Alzaneen - Gaza, Unknown Fate

09:06 AM

I put this on FB. More than 100 people saw the last one.

Mon, Nov 13 05:28 AM

06:32 AM

https://otplink.icc-cpi.int Amira, please send all your videos here. Take any that you can. Video your living conditions. This is the International Criminal Court. They want all videos taken in Gaza.

Anything you can document send here.

I know you must be careful and are forbidden to use your cell phone.

07:28 AM

I will

08:41 AM

Tue, Nov 14 04:15 AM

The internet is very bad. Here I will try to send when it is well available

10:01 AM

Amira, there is a journalist who wants to publish your story. Can you give permission for this to happen. And also, can you send the last 2 stories in Arabic. I would like you to give permission, but still retain the rights to your story.

Wed, Nov 15 05:51 AM

I have no problem with that

Thurs, Nov 16 10:03 AM

Amira, I'm thinking about you every day

I'm OK

Thank you

Sun, Nov 19 11:16 AM

Hi Amira. Where are you

Tue, Nov 21 10:12 AM

Good evening how are you, we're fine, the phone was broken

Where are you?

11:35 AM

In Rafah, south of the Gaza Strip

Ok.

CHAPTER 13
GAZA'S CATASROPHE

Gaza is a geographical area isolated from the world.
The only open crossing and road leads to heaven

"Continuous Catastrophe Since '48 Until Today, Gaza's Catastrophe"

In the southern Gaza Strip, specifically in the city of Rafah and its west, on an area not exceeding 50 dunums, within the warehouses of UNRWA supplies, more than 20,000 Palestinians from the north and the city of Gaza itself sought refuge, fleeing the horrors of the war that destroyed and took everything, whether living or inanimate. Food sources vanished, and they came searching for a bit of safety in tents constructed with the most basic available resources, made of wood, nylon, and scraps, where they slept and sought shelter.

Life in these tents is harsh, offering no protection against severe cold, strong winds, or even light rain showers. They're scattered along the fence, inside and outside, across neighboring lands, in every corner of the place.

The '48 refugees and the diaspora camps have moved here to Gaza, and delegations continue to arrive unabated. Like pilgrimages, they haven't ceased, but sadness, fear, and collapse shroud the faces of these displaced individuals.

I've seen men crying and shouting, women with reddened eyes on the verge of bursting from excessive crying and grief.

Who among us wouldn't feel the pain? Leaving behind homes, memories, every detail, and walking into the unknown, with no clear markers, leaving everything and setting forth. Most of us perhaps never reached this city, never thought about it, or knew anything about it, but the reality has been forced upon us.

I heard the cries of those unable to bid farewell to their loved ones, receiving news of their martyrdom, becoming part of the list of martyrs. It was astounding at first for me how we lived in that place amidst constant explosions and terror, the gunpowder looming over the city's sky. We couldn't sleep, and here, there's no sound. It resembles another city, far from the borders of this city. Life goes on, it hasn't stopped; they live it normally, or at least try to.

We've surpassed the difficulties of daily life as much as possible, a fire burning within our hearts, akin to those we light for cooking, heating water, baking bread, but the intensity of its burning within us is greater. Yet, we live in a time that's not ours, like primitives seeking alternatives, cut off from the world due to power outages, lack of communication, and internet blackout. Sometimes we can sleep, but with anxiety and intermittently. I don't know if it's the ghost of what we experienced in the first 30 days amidst the fires or if sleep was deprived of us peacefully. Some still miss it, and an unexpected explosion might snatch it away at any moment.

Life and days go by, but in an abnormal way.

The war has been prolonged, and its losses increase. We are alive, yet everything within us feels dead. We desire nothing; we live in a state of anxiety and tension, unable to think about what will come after the war. Everything in this country, and everything within us, is shattered, buried under rubble. Do I believe everything will return as it was? I don't think so. It's not like its predecessors; its impact is massive and significant. Its wound will bleed incessantly and won't heal.

Conclusion:

Gaza has always been like the phoenix rising from the ashes after burning, reborn anew. But this time, the ashes scatter, and the resurgence seems distant. There's no solution to our issue; our future is linked to the past, and tens of thousands live with an uncertain fate in the south, north, and Gaza.

Amira Alzaneen - Gaza - Palestine

Wednesday, 22-11-2023 - Day 47 of the War

06:25 AM

Thank you, Amira. Many hearts are with you.

Thu, Nov 23 06:17 AM

Sun, Nov 26 11:00 AM

How are you

Hey Darling!!!! How are you?????

Audio: "Good evening. I'm okay, a little sick. You know the virus here. My family is good. We are here in Rafah city. Everything may be well. I don't know how or when, but we hope that. How are you, how is your health, how is your day, what are you doing?"

Audio: "Hi Amira. I am so happy to hear from you. I am also a little bit sick, but I will be fine. I look forward to your messages every day. I know there is a ceasefire right now. I don't know what it means. Me and my friends are praying for you every single day, and there are many people all around the world thinking about you, and marching for you. I am always grateful to get your messages. Please give my best to your family. I hope that all the little babies are also okay. I hope that you feel well soon. I've seen on the news that it is very wet there, that it has been raining. I hope you can stay warm. Message when you can. I appreciate you, I love you, and I hope to see you again."

I wish you good health and thank everyone in the world who supports us, thinks about us and prays for us everything is devastating there is no place to go back to children are suffering from diseases and severe cold there is not enough bed to keep warm we hope everything will end soon we are very tired trying hard to be well and survive

We will keep fighting for you.

11:49 AM

And we will fight to stay

Mon, Nov 27 07:26 AM

Photo 13A: Amira with her red-haired younger brother Mohammad.

08:18 AM

I see your brother with red hair. This is in the south?

Yes in Rafah. This is Mohammad

I moved two weeks ago and forgot to tell you.

I remember

I know you are in Rafah. Some people tried to go North during the cease fire.

08:55 AM

This cannot prevent some of them from being injured.

Israel is lying. It is not safe to go North.

Tue, Nov 28 12:50 PM

Very tired, nothing here

I try and fight to stay strong It's very cold, no warm clothes

01:38 PM

You are living in the most impossible of times.

Yes

I don't think of staying in Gaza when all of this is over

I understand

Wed, Nov 29 06:42 AM

Video of many people running toward two large trucks. 0:12

Photos 13B and 13C: people walking away from trucks carry-ing what appear to be supplies.

Thu, Nov 30 03:50 PM

How's it going

04:01 PM

Amira!!!

04:16 PM

Yes 😊

05:01 PM

I fell asleep.! How are you?????

Fri, Dec 01 12:33 AM

Good

01:22 AM

Audio: "Amira, Amira, my darling Amira. I understand that you are living in the most terrible situation. I know that in many ways you don't have what you need. But I hope that sometimes you can have a moment of quiet, a moment of peace, and know that people are supporting you. I'm supporting you. I hope that it can help you a little bit, give you a little peace of mind. I can only in my mind imagine what the situation is. In truth, I don't think anyone can truly understand it unless they are there. But I understand at least that you are strong and your spirit is strong, and even though at times you are tired and feel weak, you are a really strong and wonderful woman and I think about you every single day."

06:20 AM

I am very grateful for your presence and the presence of those who feel me and support me, it's hard, but I'm trying, nothing is simple, but things can be complicated and difficult, I don't have anything.

Sun, Dec 03 05:48 PM

Tue, Dec 05 09:54 PM

Where are you Amira

Wed, Dec 06 12:36 AM

Good morning
I'm fine, but things were really bad

03:15 AM

Yes. I am seeing it on social media how bad.

05:10 AM

The financial situation is also we have nothing to buy and there is nothing

09:31 AM

Everybody has lost everything

01:46 PM

Exactly we don't have anything 🥹🥹🥹

Fri, Dec 08 02:35 AM

I want to ask you and I'm ashamed, there is no one who can help, you know, it's cold, there is no shelter, we came out with nothing and we need to buy a mattress and clothes to keep warm

06:39 AM

Is there a way to buy things?

I did not know you could buy things or receive money. How much do you need? And how do you receive money?

Sun, Dec 10 04:21 AM

It can be true that there are high prices in everything, but Western Union can be received here in the south they work

What you can. I can't pinpoint anything

Never be ashamed to ask. I did not know you could buy supplies. I will see what I can do.

Photo 13B

Photo 13A

Photo 13C

CHAPTER 14
WHEN ALL FEELS LOST

We are still here searching for life as much as we can.

Mon, Dec 11 04:03 AM

I was writing

04:04 AM

I feel lost and empty. I've lost my passion for everything worth yearning for in this life, which has been deprived from us for over 64 days. I lack the ability to attempt to live it normally or to continue; I have no desire to write or communicate, to follow the news, or to know all of it, burdened on the heart and exhausting for all that's within us.

Living in the unknown has become a habit. We accidentally learn some things, yet we neither cry nor are shocked or saddened. We can't muster any reaction, as if all emotions have extinguished, but within us, they burn. It stole from us our lives, routines, habits, comforts, memories, and homes - all that was ours.

I've stopped writing for a while; no words assist me, no adequate vocabulary to describe the state I live in every day. I've become impoverished, barely expressing a small part of what we're going through.

The scenes I witness daily bring tears to the eyes, yet they refuse to fall. Thousands are displaced, tents everywhere, the sound of explosions returns, and the unsettling planes persist. People still flock by the thousands to the south from all areas of Gaza. Cars and trucks filled with mattresses, this small city is insufficient and unable to contain this continuous influx, establishing small camps everywhere, on vacant land, seeking shelter and safety.

Pale faces, death drawn on them, containing a thousand questions: Where to? How? When? What will we do? What's next? Goods are not sufficiently available, and the war merchants, merciless, multiply the suffering manifold with soaring prices.

We are ashamed of our need, hesitant to ask anything from anyone because no one knows the condition of another and their capabilities. Houses and shelters are all crowded with refugees. We yearn for our lives in all its details, but will it return to normalcy and continue? I doubt it; the impact of these specific days won't fade.

Here I am in a place I don't recognize, and with the passing days, I become accustomed to a state other than my own and to circumstances I'm not used to. Forced upon us against our will, there's no resilience, no strength, no possibility of doing anything. We haven't surrendered, but even the mightiest soldiers yearn for rest. I haven't complained, but truly we're tired and have aged.

Monday / 11-12-2023 Amira Alzaneen

09:06 PM

Amira, keep writing, keep sending. I know it is tough. I want to publish it. I want to help with some money. I will let you know.

Tue, Dec 12 12:08 AM

I will

12:07 PM

Amira, I am raising some money for you from family.

Wed, Dec 13 02:42 AM

Oh thank you so much

Please thank them very much on my behalf and extend my regards and deep gratitude to them

04:02 AM

Yes. I will.

04:17 AM

🤍

🤍

06:17 AM

Thu, Dec 14 03:23 AM

Good morning

07:32 AM

Good morning. I am working on raising funds. I should have them soon.

10:51 AM

Well I can wait just be okay

Fri, Dec 15 09:46 PM

Hi Amira. I have been advised to seek help from a legal organization to be able to send money to you. I am told that some people in USA that send money have been accused of sending money to Hamas just for sending money to help Gaza. Sometimes they go to prison. Yes, it is terrible. I am contacting an American Arab organization to help me send the money. It might take a few days. I am very sorry. But I have it and will send it as soon as I can. I will send. Please wait. I am sorry. But you will receive it as soon as possible.

Sat, Dec 16 11:16 AM

It's okay, I understand that, and I apologize very much, per-haps it is better

12:26 PM

No no no. I will send it. I have it. I simply must find the way. People sent money for you.

01:05 PM

OK no problem

The only method here that I know of is Western Union, and I do not know of its problems

02:12 PM

No, it's not about Western Union, it's about that I'm verified why I sending money and who I'm sending it to, so that's what it is.

Yes I understand

I am tired and stressed, I feel tired. I want to run away.

02:44 PM

I wish you could run away. I wish I could come grab you and bring you here.

I wish that too so much.

Tue, Dec 19 01:36 PM

How are you

02:12 PM

Good I will be sending money in a couple hours. You will be able to pick it up tomorrow.

I will be sending...

02:25 PM

No problem, I'm fine. The connection had been cut off for two days and I was without internet. I was trying to rest

I can't imagine. I am imagining you healthy and strong. I will continue to help as much as possible.

I try as much as possible to stay that way because what comes next requires great strength

It does. I will make a stronger energy and effort to imagine your strength every day. You are a remarkable woman.

Your presence and support is so great to me

I care for you very much.

03:00 PM

💜

Wed, Dec 20 09:53 AM

261-######## This is your number for picking up the money.

Thu, Dec 21 10:15 AM

Good evening, thank you very much. I will try to spend it when the communication networks are restored

CHAPTER 15
I AM AMIRA

I don't know when that good morning will come,
but what I know is that today's sun has risen while we are alive,
but the good is buried

10:40 AM

I wrote a text that I would like to publish

Thu, Dec 21 10:40 AM

Hello,

I'm Amira from Gaza.

Today, I was at the market, wandering in search of some necessities. On my way, I came across a journalist asking passersby: 'What are your wishes for the new year?' The question wasn't directed at me yet, but I closed my eyes, and in a few fleeting seconds, all that happened over the tragic 76 days flashed before me. That journalist's voice woke me, and I told him I'd be honest in my answer.

A message to the world: We're here, and we've become afraid of wishes. We sleep not knowing if there will be a new tomorrow. We don't think much about the coming year. We're unable to grieve and cry; we don't know what the days hold, or if there will be a new year. We desire it to be filled with hope to ease the pain we've lived through this year.

Not a home is spared from sorrow, pain, and loss. Our hopes shattered, our aspirations and dreams stolen. We desire a life like life, to be seen by the world as humans deserving to live, to permanently stop this war, to cry and mourn for all that happened.

We haven't thought about the future, only the day we live. My tears almost fell, but I held back. I replied to the question: 'How was this year?' I couldn't find words to describe it except as filled with tragedy and bitterness. But I wonder, will it pass, or will there be no new tomorrow?

Amira Alzaneen Thursday, 21/12/2023

Thank you. I will work on this.

You received the money?

Not yet

Ok. let me know.

Communications are still cut off since yesterday and offices are not working

Ok.

I will

Tue, Dec 26 10:26 AM

Where are you

Fri, Dec 29 05:54 PM

Hi Amira. I am thinking of you every day.

Sun, Dec 31 10:17 AM

Good evening, how are you? I apologize for the absence, but the phone broke down and there is no internet. I go to the office every day to receive the money, but it is postponed due to crowding. They suffer a lot here. I hope all this will end soon.

Oh Amira!!! I am overjoyed to hear from you.

Ok. You will receive it soon. I also know there are many trucks at the Rafah border waiting to deliver supplies. The world is still vigilant about Palestine.

I love you.

My dear and great Jeannie, my closest and affectionate friend and like a mother to me, I wanted to write some words to you on the occasion of the New Year. I am very proud of the presence of a person like you in my life, and I am even grateful for the days that brought us together. I hope that we will have a meeting soon in the New Year that fulfills wishes, full of happiness and opportunities, and everything is better and peace prevails. And love and spend a beautiful time among your loved ones

Happy Christmas

10:52 AM

Dearest Amira, thank you. Feel that you are equally important to me. You give me reasons to strive, to be a better and better version of myself. We will see each other. We will let God the greatness of the universe, figure this out. Always much love. Your strength, even in the lowest moments, is a testament to what is great in a Palestinian. You have it. Even when those around you may fail to be strong in love and kindness. You are.

These beautiful words mean a lot to me, they give me all the love and kisses

Yes. They do. For you.

You received the money. I hope it helps a little. What is the situation? Is there anything it can help you with

Thu, Jan 11 04:41 AM

Amira!!

Good evening how are you

Hey there!!!

12:41 PM

Yes I received it and I was want to tell you but my phone is broken

I got the message from Western Union. I sincerely hope it helps you

Of course help me I pay some clothes and many things and food

Thank God.

02:07 PM

I'm here

03:31 PM

Fri, Jan 12 10:23 AM

Sorry for the lack of communication, but the internet was bad and the phone was down. Thank you for everything I got and it helped me a lot in getting some things.

I understand that internet is bad. I am grateful when I can hear from you. The case against Israel for genocide against Palestinians is happening now in the International Criminal Court.

I hope that a just decision will be issued for us, that we will be treated fairly, that the war will end, and that we will live in peace soon

We all pray for this every day. Yes Amira. Thankful for all the courageous people who made this case against Israel.

The days of war have been very long. We are tired. We have no energy left. They destroyed everything. We have no home now. No dreams or anything.

CHAPTER 16
100 DAYS

You would hear me if I called out to someone alive,
but there is no life for those you call out to.
We are all postponed funerals, waiting for their turn.
We are people of determination

Fri, Jan 12 10:58 AM

100 days

Here, the deadly war on Gaza has come to reach its hundredth day. In search of safety and water, we escaped from bombing, explosions and killing at every moment. The bitter days in which death might be assassinated at any moment, there is no place to return to us. The days will pass to survive and stay after the end of the war. Will we be able to continue. Will we find something that has lost the passion for everything and was completely extinguished. I am afraid that this war will take away my life and my dreams remain stuck without reaching them?

Who knows my dreams My fear of tomorrow

I did not wish for myself

Many things are waiting for my freedom to happen, the first of which is I am afraid not to reach it

Why, but I expect the new year to come in this way Friday 12/1/2024

Amira Alzaneen

Sat, Jan 13 02:24 PM

Photo 16A: many Palestinian flags flying during the January 13 March for Palestine in Washington, DC.

02:49 PM

I hope everything ends soon

Yes. Love you Amira

All love for you

I'm sorry the internet so bad

04:00 PM

Video of Palestinian flags flying as people chant "Free free Palestine" during the March for Palestine.

Photo 16B.

Sun, Jan 14 12:05 AM

Mon, Jan 15 08:35 AM

Hi how are you :)

Hi Amira Where are you

Still in my place

09:00 AM

Send a picture of where you are

Just a moment

Ok

Photo 16C: Amira.

09:24 AM

Beautiful. Can you send pictures of where you are staying

09:47 AM

I well send

09:59 AM

I want to see the living conditions

10:14 AM

I will send a video for you now of the place, what we do now, and some pictures

Thank you

12:57 PM

Photo 16D: Amira's mattress on the ground in her tent, with clothes folded behind it. Next to the mattress is a pole that holds up the tent.

Ok

Are you in a house?

Or a tent? Or school?

01:12 PM

Photo 16E: the plastic sides of her tent.

The internet so bad

Photo 16F: outdoor oven with a burning fire, baking bread, and a basket of finished bread.

Tent

01:31 PM

I am glad you are off the ground with that mattress. Are you warm now?

Yes of course

I sent some videos, but due to poor internet access, they were late in arriving

Where is your family? Are you with anyone?

I'm with my family but everyone do some things you will see them in the video

Ok. I hope it is good with them.

Wed, Jan 17 12:33 PM

On the Internet, three days ago, I sent videos and they have not arrived yet. This is sad

02:31 PM

How are you?

I'm fine with about you??

Ok. Freezing in Washington DC

Here the cold is so intense we shiver

I know. have been reading about it. The rain. The people being ill, not enough food. We are praying that Egypt sends the aid trucks soon. I pray you stay safe and healthy.

Yes, the weather is very cold, and epidemics, diseases, influenza, and many other things have spread. The aid is not enough and does not cover the number in Rafah, and there is not enough, and even if it arrives, it is not distributed fairly, unfortunately.

Yes. I have heard this. Are you healthy now?

Yes

Brief video of Amira in her tent. 0:06

05:23 PM

You look beautiful

Thu, Jan 18 03:06 AM

Video of the oven and basket of bread. Amira narrates, "That is the bread that we eat for food, and this is the oven that we make the bread in it."

03:21 AM

Video of the outside of her tent, moving to inside the tent. Amira narrates, "This is the place that we sit in it, the tent. We live in Rafah, the south of Gaza. We sleep here, away from our home, all the day hard work. We'll make bread here in the oven." The video moves out of tent to where the oven is located outside a few meters away. "My mother fires it." The video moves to show the crowded tents everywhere, connected together. "Many people live in this place, far away from the war."

Video of Amira speaking into the camera. "Hello, how are you? Nothing new, as usual routine. I sit in the tent, we make bread for the food. My mother will bake it in the oven with the fire. This system is in our days now. We sit in the tent away from our home, hard work all the day, this is the tent, we sit in it." The video moves to show the tent interior, with all belongings neatly folded and stacked at one end. "I make this video for my friend Jeannie, for you support me and . . ." With a small laugh, the video ends.

02:00 PM

Photo 16G: three red roses, against a backdrop of crowds of people milling about.

Photos 16H and 16I: the beach and blue shoreline, with Amira's shadow as she stands there.

Photo 16J: seashells covering the sand at the beach.

Today, in an attempt to change, we walked a long distance to reach the sea, hoping for a little rest. It was a beautiful time, and then we went to the camp. There was a flower seller at the gate. I bought it to make myself happy and an attempt to beautify reality and love life and beauty.

As you should. I am praying for you and your family. That you may all have peace together.

03:13 PM

I was making a video

04:23 PM

Video of Amira's silhouette on the beach, set to beautiful music and Arabic.

Fri, Jan 19 11:37 AM

Gaza is the 105th day of the war. There is no home left and there is no safety. There is no normal life or anything normal. We are living without passion. We have been extinguished, and we have lost a lot of distance. We are still afraid, and we may have it tomorrow again.

Something deep within you lives. It is there. It is your spirit. It is still alive and strong. Maybe you don't feel it. But it is there.

I try be ok and strong all the time

You can cry. You can feel weak sometimes. The task in front

of you is enormous. I hope sometimes you can sit quietly by yourself.

I can't I feel that I want to cry but I can't

I understand. I think you do not feel safe to cry.

When we cry, we feel many things. Then we think, how do I stop crying? What can I do?

One thing I am sure of. One day you will cry.

Not this specifically, as if there are no tears left to cry, I am afraid of tomorrow

I can see what you mean exactly. Yes. Whatever you do or feel now, or don't feel, is the right thing. We cannot begin to imagine your circumstances. We cannot begin to imagine how you wait for the world to help you.

I want you to know that I feel you every day. I think about you every day. Yesterday in the grocery store I showed a stranger your video of the ocean and told her it was Gaza. I am here. I will continue to help.

12:21 PM

When I cry, I explode, as if everything that was hurting me came at once, and my heart is torn out of its place and in severe pain

Is it frightening?

Yes, what is scary is losing someone, more destruction, not knowing anything, continuing the war, everything is scary, having our lives stolen in an instant is terrifying.

Your presence by my side, your support, and your thinking of me makes me strong and reassures me that you tell the world about me and my story so that I do not remain unknown. I want everyone to know that I have dreams and a love for life, and to know me, love me, and help me. I want to live. If I go and die, do not make me just a number. Talk about me a lot.

Yes. It is.

I do. And I will continue to do so.

Love to you Amira. I am here.

Love you so much

Thank you. My dear.

I am the one who should thank you for everything

If there is someone who can help us, that would be good. You know, we lost everything and were left in a faraway place, and when we return, there is no place left, no house, nothing left.

No. Amira always know how valuable you are.

In this, we will need to raise a lot of funds. It will cost very much, and we will work with others to make that happen.

I trust that God will not abandon us and everything will be fine and we can work on it. We hope that this war will end very soon

Me too.

Sat, Jan 20 08:02 AM

Oh Mahmoud, there is no longer anything on this earth worthy of life. Rather, there is no longer anything called life. On this earth, death, destruction, blood, and violence surround us from all sides. Fear sits on our pillows and looms over our nights. Our dreams were stolen and assassinated in cold blood. Kills The heart and extinguish the soul, Mahmoud. They put a barrier between us and the life we deserve. All things have become faded. The colors have become the walls, the streets, the clouds, the sounds, the music, the buildings, the cars. Everything is dull, silent, and frightening. The stillness of death. The mother of the martyr is undulating forcibly over who she said goodbye to, and another is crying blood from her wounded man, and a child is trembling in terror. One man has lost his source of livelihood and does not know where to start, the falafel seller is sad, the bookstore owner is sick, and the children curse the occupation a thousand times.

How will that rubble be replaced and the ashes removed? We have left everything behind us for an unknown destination, and we are here praying to God to have mercy on us and to restore to us what our souls lost, or we are waiting for our turn to become stories. It is narrated and told about. We search for some calm and safety. Our hearts tremble from the shocks. We ask God not to burden us with what we cannot bear. Do you think it is a nightmare and will it end?? Or will we have to wait longer??

Saturday 1/20/2024 Amira Alzaneen

Photo 16A

Photo 16B

Photo 16C

Photo 16D

Photo 16E

Photo 16F

Photo 16G

2:00 PM

Photo 16H

Photo 16I

Photo 16J

2:04 PM

CHAPTER 17
THE COLD AND RAIN, CHILDREN AND KITTIES

Job's patience is no longer a story, it is actually lived and seen 💔
Trying to find beauty amidst the enormous amount of suffering

Wed, Jan 24 01:39 PM

Hi how are you

02:07 PM

Hi Amira

How are you :)

Hi I am ok.

I'm glad to hear from you. I want to tell you to keep writing to me.

I'm OK and my family too but we are frozen here. I will write ✏️ as I can all the time don't worry and I wish this war end very soon

It is very cold. I am sorry. Please write. Thank you. Write about the cold.

A Cold Winter

But it does not compare to the coldness of our hearts.

Everything around us is cold and makes us feel frozen. Our bodies are trembling here in the camp. There is nothing to be afraid of, the freezing cold. There are not enough clothes or bedding to warm us. Even the tents made of wood and nylon are useless, from which drops of water fall as a result of held breaths. Due to the overcrowding of the place, we sleep close to each other in search of some warmth, and in order for the existing bed to be sufficient for more than 15 people, we cannot provide enough to cover everyone. We share everything, bedding, covers, and the sleeping place. We have lost the luxury of life. Things are a little good without the rain falling, which makes things worse. We loved winter and rain, but now we always pray for it not to rain so that we drown in water and everything gets wet. We only have a little. Our warm homes are gone and the beautiful winter seasons that we were accustomed to. Evenings, drinks, and warm and hot food. There is none of them. We use fires to cook this food. Even if we have it, our hearts have frozen due to so much of what we have lived. Fear subsides. In every breath, even those tears froze in our eyes. Not only is the winter cold, but we are cold because of the abundance of pain and pain and the amount of loss and bereavement. It is not the winter that makes us cold, but rather the world froze and did nothing for us to stop the massacres and death that does not leave us, and add to that the diseases that we are suffering from due to the lack of food and medicine. And climate changes and the extreme cold. Many young children were killed by the cold. This small city cannot accommodate this amount of people and what is in it is not enough for all of them. Is there anyone who feels for us, helps us, extends a helping hand to us, brings back the details and memories and what we lost? We are here now, and after a moment we may no longer be;

Amira Alzaneen

Orphan Gaza

Photo 17A: looking outside from the tent flaps onto puddles of water and bleak light.

Photo 17B: clouds above tops of tents; a covered moon illuminating a dark blue-gray sky, lighting the tops of the lower clouds in pale pink.

03:34 PM

Thank you.

Love to you.

Thu, Jan 25 03:49 AM

04:05 AM

Good morning how are you. My friend do something for me, look

Amira sends a link to a GoFundMe site made by a friend in Germany.

06:28 AM

This is.good.

This will help you a lot. But don't take all the money at once. How did you meet her?

06:49 AM

I know about that

I know her on social media from a long time from my writing

07:58 AM

From Facebook?

11:48 AM

Yea

Yes

Excellent

12:40 PM

I have a new story to tell you

Today, someone came looking for me asking for help. Her name is Shannen. She is Canadian, married to a Palestinian. She fled the city in Khan Yunis after the Jews expelled them. She is trying to leave Gaza, but it is impossible to do so without her husband because he does not have citizenship, and she refuses to leave without him. She came. She needs to write to the Canadian embassy for help. She will tell me her story so that I can publish it.

Tomorrow she will come back to tell me

01:02 PM

I will include it.[3]

---

3 Unfortunately, I think this woman never returned to see Amira.

Fri, Jan 26 01:19 PM

01:33 PM

It's raining

Audio of pouring rain.

Alot

Oh dear.

Are you dry

Is your tent strong enough

Video of the tent ceiling as it sags with the rain. Sounds of dripping are heard.

I'm not sure about that to be honest this the first time it raining like that

I hope it stops. Soon.

I hope that to

At normal days I love the winter so much and raining but now we feel very cold

Yes. I agree completely.

Our home in winter was wonderful full of warmth, safety and love, and these are not our homes now

No. They are your shelters. Not your homes. What happened to the kitties?

A bad story they still in the north and now we don't know anything about them

Yes. I understand. You tried. You did well.

You know, when we went out towards the south, we were forbidden from taking anything we had, so they stayed at home with someone, and then she and her children were lost. This is sad. I feel guilty for not being able to bring them with me.

But my family was careful with them, Mira, as they were in Rafah before there were any checkpoints

Amira, you did well.

Photo 17C: white cat sleeping on a pink pillow in the tent.

She is sleeping

I'm afraid that when we come back we won't find them

You won't. They were tiny baby kittens. But you have this beautiful cat. Amazing.

Yes

Did the kittens belong to this cat? No....

Today I took many pictures of everyone to send to Osama in the north

No, there is another mother who stayed with them called Sukka, a brunette

Osama is in the North???? Your brother???

Photos 17D and 17E: a beautiful red-headed boy, ten years old, wearing a blue jacket.

1/26/24,

Yusef

He is a beautiful boy.

Yes, unfortunately he, Osama, his wife, his son, and some of my uncles, their wives, and their families stayed in the north. He was unable to leave

They are ok?

Photo 17F: Amira's mother in front of the makeshift outdoor oven, other family members looking on.

Photo 17G: a one-year-old boy playing in the sandy dirt, a young woman in the background.

I did not know Osama was married.

My mother and my sister Aseel are making bread in the clay oven, and the child, Sanad, my sister's son, Warda, and behind him is my sister Fidaa, whom you know

May I post the children in social media

No, on the contrary, you know that I met his wife and son, Hassan Al-Saghir, while you were visiting me at home

Oh yes!!!!

I will definitely send you more in a moment

Photo 17H: a little five-year-old girl looking sadly up at the camera. She is wearing a printed blue sweatshirt, gray sweatpants, and one sandal and one slipper, both too big.

She is Jorey my little sister

Photos 17I and 17J: a red-headed twelve-year-old boy with freckles, smiling and laughing.

This is Mohammad, you remember him and Yusuf, the two red boys, my brothers

Today the international criminal justice court voted 15 to 2 that Israel was committing genocide. The only countries voting against were Israel and Uganda.

It is the start of victory.

Sat, Jan 27 12:34 AM

Photo 17K: six young children together. One red-headed girl looks about twelve; with her are twelve-year-old Muhammad and five younger children, the youngest being the one-year-old.

Photo 17L: red-headed girl flashing a peace sign with her fingers while standing in front of a tent.

Photo 17M: the one-year-old on the lap of a woman with a scarf over her head, barefoot, the makeshift oven on the bare dirt in the background.

Video of the one-year-old boy in socks in front of a tent, taking his first steps into the arms of the smiling Mohammad. Three other children smile proudly.

Photos 17N and 17O.

Photo of a young man, looking down as he stands on the bed of a truck with a laundry basket, a dirty yellow three-gallon jug on its side, some cooking utensils, and a metal coffee pot.

We hope 🙏

Sorry the internet was off

This [the red-headed girl in the photos] is Aileen, my cousin, who looks like us. She lost her father during this war

This little Sanad takes his first steps and the children are happy for him

Wed, Jan 31 05:42 AM

Hi how are you

I just woke up.

What is happening today Amira

05:58 AM

I don't know yet

The internet was destroyed we couldn't know anything in the news

You are in your tent now

Yes

Is it raining

No, sunshine

Photos 17P and 17Q: selfies of Amira.

06:39 AM

Still beautiful. I don't know if this helps. But you are beautiful.

Oh thanks beautiful like you

Photo 17R: a white plastic bag tied to a pole along the ceiling of the tent.

Photo 17S: selfie of Amira.

07:53 AM

Sad. Beautiful

10:30 AM

Photo 17T: a cup of coffee.

Thu, Feb 01 02:40 AM

I love that you have coffee!!!

Me to feel happy so much

What is in the bag?

Some Medical tools and medicines, first aid

Ok. How is your physical health? Are you receiving enough food?

Good yes we have

03:10 PM

Not enough but we have

Yes. I have seen that there is not enough food.

Nothing to do thanks God for everything

You. In a place taking everything. Waiting for the good in the world to be stronger than the evil to show itself.

I hope that there will be justice and eliminate evil, and I hope that peace will return soon. Everything is starting to be implemented now. Tomorrow we may not find it. You know how it will be.

I imagine only one way. I imagine only the way of rebuilding.

I don't know what will happen after a moment

This is true. You must live minute by minute. Moment by moment. With the unexpected

Yes exactly

04:02 PM

Yes. And this is a stress most people would find difficult to manage. 💔

Fri, Feb 02 02:22 AM

May Allah help us

02:10 PM

Today I prepared maqluba for lunch. The weather was raining and very cold. The cat, Mira, was sleeping all the time, warming herself. We were also drinking hot coffee in bed so that we would not get sick.

A new month has come, the second of the year. I hope that there will be an end to the war and a return to peace, our homes and their lives, and an end to the genocide. We have run out of what we have and UNRWA aid may stop. It is scary. I cannot ask for help at any time. It may not be available to everyone, you know, but I pray that this will end soon.

02:37 PM

We were running like crazy in the tent because of water leaking from the ceiling inside it and for fear of its destruction due to the large amount of water accumulating on top of it.

A major problem that leads to wet bed, increased cold, and inability to sleep

I have seen pictures of people sleeping in the mud. Tents full of water.

Yes, it is not possible to prevent water from leaking into the tent when it rains, and the sleeper does not feel it. He is tired and looking for comfort and warmth. It is not possible to fix everything.

Yes. The world is watching. Spain has pledged aid to UNRWA. Some countries have cut aid, but only those aligned with Israel.

Yes, I heard about that, but this is a major disaster if the aid provided by them stops, as life now depends on it other than that which cannot reach northern Gaza, and Gaza City is suffering from hunger and destruction, and the situation here will become the same if it stops.

Yes. The evil in America is trying hard. But many good are also working hard.

We still hope all this will end very soon

Me too. And the rebuilding begins. There is much to do.

03:30 PM

It still raining 😷😷
Audio of steady rainfall. 0:20

03:50 PM

Video of the ceiling of the tent, dark-blue patches visible where the rain has soaked through.

Sat, Feb 03 12:16 PM

Hello, how are you? I hope you are well. Ashamed, I ask to search for help again, but this time to send it to my brother Osama in northern Gaza so that he can buy the necessary food and drink.

12:34 PM

I know everyone needs help but I prefer help Osama

Mon, Feb 05 03:34 AM

I'm sorry if this difficult

09:00 AM

I'm sorry I am sick. I just got back into bed.

10:17 AM

Oh sorry to know that

10:41 AM

Oh it's ok. Just a little slow. Where is Osama now?

10:52 AM

Audio: "Hello, good evening, how are you. I wish your health, uh, will be back very soon and you will be okay and fine. Osama is in the North now, um, behind Beit Hanoun, our city. He's sit in the school. He cannot come to here, and we cannot go to there. We wish the war will end very soon and come back for our homes and see them, and Osama, and his wife, and his son Hassan. We hope that."

Tue, Feb 06 06:41 AM

Two selfies of Amira.

[112] AMIRA ALZANEEN AND JEANNIE AMASH

Photo 17A

Photo 17B

Photo 17C

Photo 17D

Photo 17E

Photo 17F

Photo 17G

Photo 17H

Photo 17J

Photo 17I

Photo 17K

Photo 17L

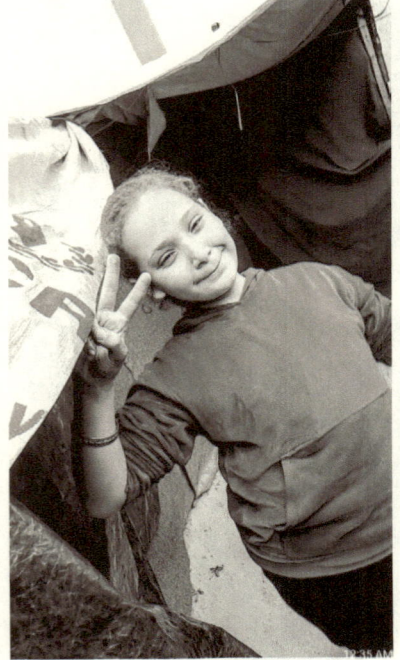

Photo 17M

Photo 17N

Photo 17O

Photo 17P

Photo 17Q

Photo 17R

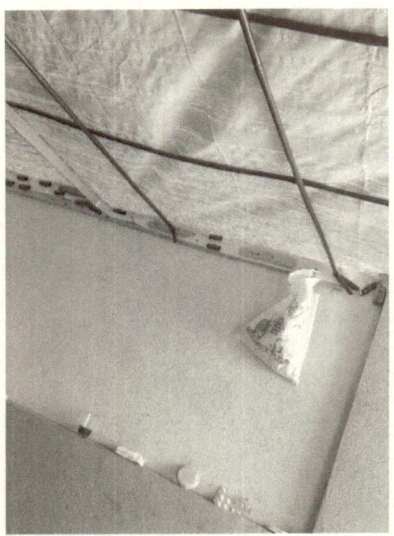

Photo 17T

Photo 17S

CHAPTER 18
A NEW NIGHTMARE LOOMS

Butterflies will fly at my funeral, and the words of the elderly and children who I once smiled at or helped carry a burden will follow me. All those I rescued from darkness will remember me, and all those I loved and who loved me will know that my impact is eternal, and that, though simple, it will last for the rest of their lives. They will smile and say: He has returned to his homeland, there, where good souls and peace are.

06:54 AM

I write a new thing

Yes? Good! Let me see!

Absolutely

Just a moment I will translate it

Ok

Tue, Feb 06 07:14 AM

A new nightmare looms on the horizon.

It's Tuesday, the 6th of February, 2024, the 124th day of the war on Gaza.

The fires of war still rage in this city, unabated and intensifying day by day. Destruction and casualties increase relentlessly, compounded by widespread famine and diseases due to the massive influx and overcrowding of displaced persons. The city lacks basic necessities for life: no potable water, insufficient food, inadequate shelter from the winter cold. What little aid exists is scarce and inaccessible to many, with most places rendered uninhabitable. Explosions, attacks, and massacres persist throughout this once vibrant city, now reduced to rubble resembling a ghost town. We never imagined living like this, cut off from each other completely, with no safe passage, no respite from the siege tightening around us.

Every thought of the enemy's encroachment fills us with a thousand deaths in a single moment. We fled in search of safety, but it seems too much to hope for. If no one intervenes to stop this catastrophe, it will lead to a massive genocide and even greater terror than before. The psychological toll mounts as we face the constant fear of becoming victims at any moment. There is no life left in us, only endurance, striving to survive in whatever way we can, knowing that an even greater war lies ahead after this brutal conflict ends.

Nothing changes, our voices unheard, our souls free-flowing like a river of blood with no one to stem its tide. Our cries go unanswered, our pain unacknowledged. Will this fear ever end?

We once had lives, stolen from us in their entirety. The slow death is more agonizing than the instant cessation of life. The stories are too numerous, our energy too depleted to tell them anymore. Heart-wrenching sighs betray the depth of our suffering. All we can do is pray, for God is our only savior.

Our eyes, wells of tears, narrate our tragedies. Our homeland, though besieged, remains dear, and our people, though doubted, retain their dignity. We've lost everything—family, friends, homes—dispersed, never to reunite. They were buried without farewells, without tears, without condolences. We once believed in the goodness of all, but our trust was misplaced, our disappointment compounded.

May God forgive you all, for we will be your adversaries on the Day of Judgment. To those who brought us to this state, may you never know peace. Our days blur into oblivion, wishing for death with every moment. The heart overflows, words failing to express the magnitude of our suffering. We've aged a hundred years in a single day. Hasn't that been enough to halt all this?

I am Amira Alzaneen

From Gaza, the land that quenches the world's thirst for freedom, honor, and humanity with dignity, patience, resilience, and strength. We inscribe history, alter equations, and engrave the Palestinian cause into every mind and place. We are the children of beloved Palestine, born from Gaza, destined to rise from every burning, breathing life amidst the ashes.

08:02 AM

This is bringing me to tears. This. Is. Your. True. Gift.

08:30 AM

Were you studying Media and Communications at school?

We are going to submit your work to an online publication called Counterpunch. They would like a short biography of you. They will not take the rights. I want to see if I can monetize your work. This magazine might be a good introduction. We will get your work out there Amira.

Oh I can make short video about that Talking about my self

Something like: Amira is a young woman from Gaza who was completing her studies at Palestine University when the latest assault in Gaza began. She fled to the Rafah, witnessing cruel horrors along the way. She is currently living in an UNRWA tent in Rafah with her surviving family.

Yes, you can make a video.

I will

09:56 AM

Audio: "This will be very good. I study media and communication at the University of Palestine. You know that I am not finished my studying yet. I love writing. I write all the situation that I have been, live in it in Gaza, exactly in this war."

Audio: "I can't make a video. I am crying when I speak about everything that I live. I will send a voice message like that, this will be better."

Tue, Feb 06 10:01 AM

Hello, My Name is Amira Alzaneen, from Gaza, Palestine.

I am 26 years old. I studied media and communication at the University of Palestine. I was preparing for the beginning of the new semester when this war on Gaza began. We escaped death several times. We moved to more than one place to search for safety and peace, in Al-Shifa Hospital in the Al-Daraj neighborhood and other places. Places in Gaza, but with the intensity of the explosions everywhere and their proximity, we decided to head to southern Gaza, the place that was described as a safe zone. This will be done by walking through the corridor that was described as safe, but it is full of soldiers who point their weapons over your head and may explode them at any moment. Destruction everywhere. Some scenes are not...it can't be described when I remember it. I want to cry a lot, but I cannot. Some of the corpses lying on the road for several days. You walk slowly, raising your hands. You cannot move your eyes to the right or left. Any movement poses a great danger to your life. We walked a long distance, more than 15 kilometers, to reach Bureij and then Rafah. We left with nothing, just some clothes. We arrived and began the journey of searching for shelter in this city. We made a tent with few means to stay in. No bed, no clothes. The cold is severe, hunger, and more diseases. I do not know what our mistake is. I am a human being with the right to life and I have dreams, and everyone must respect that. We are just victims. Here I always ask myself a question: Did we deserve all this? I write the details, texts, stories, and events that we lived through to be my messages to the world to stop everything and think about us and know what we are living and so that my texts will be a memory for everyone in the event that I die too. Talking will not be enough and very little, but we are tired and I am amazed at our strength and our lack of crying. We deserve life. Life is free, safe, love and peace, and everyone deprives us of that

Audio: "The internet was so bad I decide to write the message like that. I try to have a video or a voice, but you know [small laugh] the internet here so bad. If you need anything, tell me and I will do it."

Audio: "I try to have video and talking about everything in it, but uh, you know, I cannot do that. I was trying, but I cannot imagine anyone in my place imagine what do we live. I ask myself a question, I don't know. How do we survive from all of this? How do we live our life? How we can continue with in our life? I don't know. Many questions now in my head. [Deep sigh, loud exhale.] What? Thanks for God for everything. I wish the war will end very soon and we will be back for our life."

Audio: "Another thing I want to be talking about is that we are here in Rafah in the South of Gaza. This is the place they say is safe. I am with my family. They are more than fifteen members; most of them, women and children, live in a tent. You know about that. The more details you need, ask me about that and you know I will answer."

Audio: "My message for everyone reading my writing: I want you, I want from you, to decision that you are in my place. Imagine what we live. Thinking like us when we live all of that. Do you want this war to continue? Everything to still be like that? Do you want everything in this city will die? I don't know, but I want from you to ask yourself this, all this question, and answer about it."

Audio: "We lose people that we love them, we lose our home, our favorite place, our friends, our life, our dreams, we lose everything."

Audio: "I will go somewhere to help a family. They are from Khan Younis. They don't have any bed, any clothes, we take some from us to give for them. May Allah help us, sit with us, that everything will be okay."

10:43 AM

01:33 PM

01:50 PM

I have put into motion the publication of your work. I am forming a team to help me. We will do it.

I hope everything be well

I think a book.

Because but is a Gazan Catastrophe, Holocaust.

Audio: "That will be amazing. [Laughs.] Just thinking that my work will be in the book, everyone can read it. Everyone can know our stories, everyone know what we have, what the situation is, what we live. It is making me very happy, very proud. I think of continuing with my writing. You know I hope everything will be okay and start to be very well."

Audio: Israeli drone can be heard overhead. "Also, I think after the situation will be back for our life, be good, be safety, in this I think to write about my experience in the life. You know, marriage and like that, and what happened to me, after divorce, before divorce, the woman in Arab society, you know that. I think about that, but uh, not now. In the future if I'm still alive."

Is it possible to stop the war??

Is it possible that we will continue to live until the war stops?
Is it possible that we would die from shock if the war ended?

Is it possible that we are treated for our psychological ill-nesses caused by war?

Is it possible that we still have bricks to build and rebuild our homes after the war stopped?

Is it possible for our lives to return to normal?

Is it possible for our dreams to continue and our wishes to come true?

05:53 PM

Wed, Feb 07 08:06 AM

Everything will be good

We pray

10:47 AM

Thu, Feb 08 01:20 AM

Good morning

How are you

I'm fine

I am glad.

You are beautiful

Like you

Thank you.

How are you

07:47 AM

Hi Amira, I am well now. I would like you to think about how you want the book to look.

08:07 AM

We will work together.

Audio: "Absolutely. Anything you want to know, you can ask me about it and I can answer, and I hope everything will be very very good."

I love you. Your voice will be heard.

08:35 AM

Audio: "I love you to ever. You are like my angel, my best friend, my big support woman, and I wish one day I will be like you, have a good voice for the world to hear, have a good idea, a good support for others."

09:08 AM

Audio: "You will. One day you will."

04:56 PM

Can you write to me the story of how you began University and your scholarships. Then the story of how your brother was shot by Israel and how you stopped to care for him.

Sat, Feb 10 05:19 AM

Absolutely I can

06:01 AM

Thank you. Yesterday I went to the library and used their computer. I began copying your little writings and printed a few pages. I am amazed at how beautiful is your writing, all over again. We will need a translator. Sometimes Google translate is not perfect. I will look for someone. This is a big and beautiful project. 🤍

This is a start.

Sat, Feb 10 08:48 AM

The beginning

After the release of my high school results for the year 2015, I passed with a good grade. Despite my family's bad circumstances, which would not enable me to study at the university and afford its expenses, I did not give up and began the journey of searching and registering at the university. I aspired to study language translation, a specialty that I could not find in the universities of Gaza. I have loved writing for many years, reciting poetry, etc., so the major I was closest to was studying media and communication. I registered at the University of Palestine for a bachelor's degree. I was very enthusiastic and had a great passion and love for practice and learning. The teachers loved my energy and diligence and this great enthusiasm. I applied what I studied at the university in a direct practical way and it grew. This is my ability to write and create more and more broadly, and my understanding and information increased. I studied for about a year and a half, three semesters, which I finished with an excellent and very good grade. I had a small job as a secretary in an office through which I could pay some of my university fees. However, a catastrophe happened to me that changed the course of my life. In 2018, my eldest brother Osama, was injured in his leg during the return Marches by the occupation. He was the breadwinner for our family due to my father's illness and his suffering from a bullet in his back since the intifada that prevented him from working. Our lives began to get worse and worse. I looked for all ways to treat Osama and I was then forced to leave the university and postpone it. My classes were cancelled due to the accumulation of fees, the inability to provide what was needed, the great needs of the house, and the search for additional work so that I could support them. Osama was subjected to many operations in Gaza, most of which were unsuccessful. There was a fear of his foot being amputated, so it was decided for him to travel to Egypt to begin a full medical journey. It was never that easy, as it was forbidden for anyone of his age to go out without coordination, which at the time cost an exorbitant sum estimated at $1,400 per person, in addition to housing, treatment, and transportation expenses. My mother traveled with him to support him and relieve him, and I became responsible for the house, including what was in it, and to support my 8 brothers and sisters. I stopped studying for two years. But I did not give up. I still had a dream to finish and obtain the university degree that most of my generation had preceded me. During Osama's treatment journey, I knew many friends from different cities in the world who helped us and stood with us, including my dear Jeannie, who did not leave me for a day and was the biggest supporter and encourager for me to return to university. I was able to do that in the year 2021, and I finished another year and a half of university, with about two semesters and a few hours remaining. I went through some other difficult circumstances that stopped my studies for a while, including my suffering in my life and many problems. I decided to return and continue studying despite that, but unfortunately the war on Gaza began and was stopped. All my dreams again, which seem to remain parked until the last hope. My life is not rosy, but full of suffering and an attempt to remain strong to continue. Reaching is not a simple and easy matter, but rather a road full of stumbles and repeated falls to stand up and try again, and so I cannot stay on the ground, but rather continue to stand after every time I fall into it.

Amira Alzaneen

09:04 AM

Audio: *"Sometimes I want to come back for my memories and look what I was writing. When I saw that, I can know that I can continue with my writing professionally, and in a good way, and good things. I love that, and I hope that what we want will be very good, very beautiful. And I was thinking. If something happens to me in this war, if I died, if I injury, or anything like that, you have all my story. Let the world know what I have, what we live, what we do. I think like that."*

09:16 AM

. yes Amira.

10:39 AM

http://www.instagram.com/reel/C3GTmi5OeV3/?utm_source=ig_" HYPERLINK "http://www.instagram.com/reel/C3GTmi5OeV3/?utm_source=ig_"/?utm_source=ig_ ton_share_sheet&igsh=ODdmZWVhMTFiMw==

Instagram post of a brilliant boy who took random wires and parts and bult a fan/windmill and used batteries to power electricity in his tent. Go watch it!

11:12 AM

Yes I know about him

Sun, Feb 11 02:01 AM

What happened with you about the help for Osama???

03:26 AM

Photo 18A: a cup of coffee.

04:16 AM

It is a funny and very sad thing. Finally, after nearly four months, I ate a little chocolate. On normal days before the war, it was always available at a low price, but now we only find it rarely and at a high price. This piece's price exceeded 8 dollars, and it was less than two dollars. I have a treasure. Happy and sad about our situation, like... The hungry people who do not find anything to eat, our situation is very poor and sad

Photo 18B: a Galaxy chocolate bar.

07:46 AM

Hi Amira, it is difficult for me to say that in this moment I do not have funds for Osama. I will tell you if that changes. I have sent out everything I had available to everyone I could. How is he able to purchase things?

08:00 AM

It's okay. I trust that God will make everything become better. He can.

There are some goods still available in northern Gaza, but they are expensive due to the stock and merciless merchants.

Wed, Feb 14 09:57 AM

How are you

10:36 AM

I am at the library. I am working on the book.

10:48 AM

Audio: "Oh, that's good. I want to tell you that a friend of yours, his name is Bob, sent me a message on Facebook and talked

with me about the book. He is happy, and I'm happy and proud to work with him. I wish everything will be good and will be a success. What you need from me, I'm ready to do it."

Great news! Yes, I am building a team to help.

Just keep writing!!

Audio: "It's a good team, a beautiful team. I wish success in our work. I will still keep writing about many things. [Sigh.] Today I was speaking with Osama in the North. He is in a bad situation. There is nothing to eat. No bread, no food, no vegetables. Nothing they can do, can't find something to eat. This is miserable, but I pray to be okay and good, and this war will end very soon. I hope that."

11:22 AM

Is this the same story?

Yes, the first one

Wed, Feb 14 12:37 PM

A whole day late because there was no internet.[4]

– 6:00 AM In the Land of the Phoenix that Never Dies.

Morning came, and with it, the daylight that soothes the eyes a bit because you can move around and know what's happening around you, unlike the long night where you're detached from everything except the sound of strikes, fear everywhere, and the dread of the next strike.

Where to? And we wake up to news. We've relocated many times because the danger got closer. Our current shelter is in "Nas and Nis" school. We took a classroom to shelter 19 people, four families, with less than two meters for each family.

---

4 The following is a repeat from an entry from November 3, 2023. It was repeated here, with a few changes in the English. It is included because of those simple changes, even though Amira and her family had already fled from this school to Rafah.

We lie on the ground because we left isolated without being able to take anything. Yes, that's right, we took cloth for "Suka" and their five children with us because they're afraid, and their souls are at stake.

Men spend the night outside. Our morning routine, usual since sunrise, includes providing water, bread, organizing, figuring out what today's meal will be, which may not be available at all, charging batteries and phones if possible, and barely finding anything safe – neither trees, nor stones, nor animals, nor inanimate objects, nor humans, nor children wrapped in their mothers' bellies, nor hospitals, nor schools, nor cars, nor carts, not even bakeries were spared.

You're neither awake nor asleep, nor in any state or place because there's no peace. The beginning of the week doesn't differ from the end, nor does the date or the day matter. Morning comes, and there's still a new day. Yes, everything in us is subdued, but as long as we open our eyes, it means we're still alive. We're not okay, but we're still alive. We're checking on ourselves because at any moment, we could become another number in the list of the missing. A new day, God willing, will be different. God, please grant us relief, unlike the days that passed. Have mercy on us, oh God.

We're not okay, but we're still alive. Amira Alzaneen.

Gaza – 11/2/2023.

By the way, today marks 106 years since the infamous Balfour Declaration.

Part of our daily tasks after walking nearly ten kilometers to get flour because we couldn't find bread or kitchen supplies to use.

A significant achievement despite all the exhaustion: "the smell of land or nothingness."

12:56 PM

I have two now

Photo 18A

Photo 18B

CHAPTER 19
100 QUESTIONS

I have no real wish in my heart except for God to wash away the impurities of these days of my life, to be compensated for all the hard things I lived with, to be forced as if sadness never broke me.

Wed, Feb 14 01:02 PM

One Hundred Questions

Every day, numerous questions cross my mind. It's been over 130 days since this situation began, and I wonder:

• How did all of this happen to us?

• Have we truly left our homes?

• Is this a nightmare?

• Will all of this ever end?

• Will we survive?

• Is it all just a play, ending with a comical scene after all this sorrow?

• Will we reunite with our loved ones?

• Will our lives return?

• Will we resist and reclaim our dreams?

• Do we deserve all of this?

• What have we done?

• Will they remember us, or will we be forgotten?

Truly, I know nothing, and this burdens me greatly. We used to live in great luxury, with everything we needed readily available. Then, suddenly, without warning, everything turned upside down. We lost so much and became destitute, searching for shelter, food, and clothing. If we find any, I can't accurately describe our lives currently, except to say that we've regressed to ancient times, seeking the basics of life. We're separated, with me in the south and my brother in the north of the sector. After a long period of isolation and communication breakdown, I finally spoke to them recently, and tears streamed down my face seeing their condition. At least we find our food and sustenance, but there, they're living in famine, with nothing to eat except animal feed turned into bread due to the lack of flour. There are no vegetables, and everything available is unfit for consumption or drinking. Destruction is everywhere, severe cold, deadly hunger, pale faces, and constant fear haunt them. I wished for death a thousand times.

This isn't living; it's as if life is forbidden to us, and our rights have been stolen. There's no one to advocate for us or turn to. We've lost everything living and non-living; we've regressed centuries back, unable to describe our tragedies and pains. The days of war have prolonged endlessly, and the questions multiply in my mind every day. The situation is very debilitating; I fear every moment of losing what I love. Our spirits are crushed; we can no longer continue. Our bodies await annihilation, and our souls are fragile and broken. The stories and narratives have multiplied, and I feel we'll either be a part of them or narrate them to the world. My words fail me, but we're dying slowly.

Amira Alzaneen The Desolate Gaza

CHAPTER 20
VALENTINE'S DAY

A person who is educated by experiences will not be anyone's student.

Wed, Feb 14 01:04 PM

And another one

Valentine's Day

Wednesday, February 14th, the love of Gaza. It is said that today is Valentine's Day, a day known to the whole world, but we have no love, no life. Our color red is our blood spilled on the ground, rivers of blood that have not stopped flowing for 130 days. Our limbs amputated and scattered everywhere, unnoticed by anyone, unmerciful world. We used to love life and all it contained, we loved the sunrise and its sunset. Now, we breathe with the sunrise and fear and fill with terror at sunset. Our beautiful city is gray in color, its features erased. Faces worn with fatigue and fear, eyes expressing pain. On Valentine's Day, to the whole world, from Gaza, we ask: Was our blood enough to color your Valentine's Day with its dark charm? We love our land and our homeland, so we nourish it with our blood and sacrifice it with our souls. But our condolences to you and your lost humanity.

Amira Alzaneen

No life, no love for Gaza.

Photos 20A and 20B: the oven with burning embers and a charred piece of wood halfway into the fire. A cup of coffee sits on the ground in front of the stove.

Video: The fire in the stove is roaring, with two pieces of wood feeding it. 0:12

Audio: "Good morning, dear, and how is your day? [Laugh.] That's my morning. I made fire to the water. We will make bread, you know, that is our routine every day. I hope a good day for you. I know that it's the night there."

Photo 20A

Photo 20B

CHAPTER 21
WHERE DO AN HONORABLE PEOPLE GO?

O God, I ask you not to turn off and my patience does not dry up, my days' paths get lost, my laughter does not sound, and I do not live in anxiety while you are in my heart and that I do not break at the moment when I believe in my strength, that I do not be like the one who resists the storm and is destroyed by a wind. Oh God, cleanse me from the misery of life and from every distress

Thu, Feb 15 04:11 AM

"Where do we go?"

This question, despite its simplicity, is painful with no clear answer, especially after this small city of Rafah, where over one million seven hundred thousand displaced people from all over Gaza are subjected to intense bombardment, explosions everywhere, gruesome massacres, and the killing of children and innocent people who came seeking shelter and stayed in tents thinking they were safe. This city, described by the occupation as secure, was attacked, killing peaceful civilians and civilians in their tents. The news circulated, and severe psychological warfare indicated that war was approaching this small city. The question echoed among all tongues and the sorrow in their eyes, "Where do we go?" There is nowhere to go, and they are not allowed to return to their homes. The tents no longer protect them, and the situation worsened. A small spot besieged by the Egyptian border to the south and by the occupation's armored vehicles and soldiers to the east, west, and north. We no longer own anything, and we are tired of displacement, moving from one place to another without a fixed destination. We are beginning to think that death is the solution to all this tragedy and pain. There is no clear talk about the end of this war or any change. Our pain has multiplied, and our hunger and oppression have increased. There is no place for us, and our sorrows are not acknowledged. Is safety far from us? Are we going to die in cold blood? Where do we go?

Thursday, 15-2-2024 Amira Alzaneen

Gaza, the bottom of the bottle that almost burst its last part.

Thu, Feb 15 05:07 AM

I Grew Up in a Simple Rural Life.

I wasn't used to washing by hand or scrubbing my feet until they hurt, or rubbing laundry until my hands turned blue from the cold water. I didn't learn to light a fire or cook on charcoal or wood. I learned to knead dough to bake on a griddle or in a taboon oven. I didn't grow accustomed to showering without a showerhead, using shampoo unsuitable for my hair, without conditioner or even a loofah. I didn't learn to open cans of the preserved food we use every day because we were taught they were all full of preservatives. I didn't sleep on a mattress on the floor with an uncomfortable pillow that hurt my neck and a thin mattress on cold tiles letting the cold seep into my body. I didn't drink salty or tasteless water. I didn't cook a meal once a week without meat or chicken. I wasn't used to my kids asking to be warm while I couldn't provide it. I wasn't used to my mom asking for a certain dish and me saying it's not possible because it's not available. I wasn't used to not going out for enjoyable outings with my family and sisters. I wasn't used to eating food that smelled like firewood and tasted bland. I wasn't used to working in the kitchen without having everything I needed, not just working with pots, pans, and a kettle. Oh, those days were all about dignity. May God have mercy on an honorable people. 😖

Amira Alzaneen

07:49 AM

Amira, I think I need to find a translator. There are a few places where the words are not exactly right However, part of me feels that I should leave it, as it shows how you are trying to communicate sometimes with Google translate, sometimes just trying to find the words yourself. after I finish printing off everything we have so far, I will go through all of it and check with you any changes in the language that I think are important. This is how I will begin the editing process. Much love to you. Thank you for all your work.

Audio: "You know I love English, but I have hard sometimes to write very well with it. You know my mother language is Arabic and the English I learned is British. Different, many different between it and American. I don't use Google Translate all the time. I use ChatGPT to translate the words, sometimes others."

Audio: "Yes, it's very very good, but sometimes there is a word or a sentence that I feel is not exactly what you are looking for. I'm glad you are not always using Google Translate. I'm very glad to hear this is how you mostly write, because that's better. In that regard, I think we should leave it mostly as it is, just sometimes there are places where I think it is not exactly as you meant."

This looks great

Alright!

She is very passionate about everything so that the world can understand the message and our stories

08:33 AM

You are passionate about everything!!

Yes exactly

CHAPTER 22
PAINFUL SEPARATION OF FAMILIES

When you miss your country, say I will visit the remains of the wreckage.
Here, Gaza has become like my heart with its fragments.
Say I will visit the cemetery of my loved ones

09:39 AM

Jeannie, I'm scared, and perhaps this is the first time I admit it. I'm not afraid of war or death, but I miss Osama a lot, and Hassan, the little one, I long to see him and hug him. We live in the same country, and the distance between us doesn't exceed half an hour to meet, but it's impossible because of this war and deceit. I feel like my heart stops with every piece of bad news. He is my hero, my support, and my friend, you know that. When we meet someone we haven't seen in a while because of the war, we hug them tightly to comfort them and ourselves. We can't talk much because our pains are too many. I'm afraid of the idea of not meeting, of separation, distance, hunger, thirst, and coldness. I can't do anything. I just want my brother and his family to be safe. I want our lives to return to normal again. Is this too much, and is my wish impossible?

It's been over a hundred days since I last saw them, and we haven't met. I fear when their news stops coming, and I can't contact them. That terrifies me a lot.

Yes. I understand.

10:19 AM

Photo 22A: a cup of coffee, tent interior in the background.

10:48 AM

Dark skinned mistress

Audio: "I got—[a child shouts over her voice]—inside to use the internet. I wish it was good or better than the outside. My cousin's son came from another place in Rafah, they are in a school They want—uh, their father [is] in the north with my brother Osama. He wants to talk to them and see them, a video call, using the internet, the only way to communication with each other here and there. They miss their father, they was crying. The situation, it's really very sad. But the internet so bad it cut. They say that tomorrow maybe it will be good because it's Friday, uh, he will talk to us at another time. I'm feeling very sad. They are just children. They don't know anything about everything. They don't deserve that. They asking just for, they said they need to see their father, be around, but this way be impossible! We cannot go to the north, people in the north cannot come to the south. [Frustrated sigh.] I cannot imagine the situation that we are live in it. I wish this war will end very soon, and everyone see the people they love. I hope that."

Yes

Video: people walking in the causeway between rows of tents. It is raining, the ground as glassy wet dirt.

Photos 22B, 22C.

It was raining

Where do you go to the toilet?

Oh, regarding this matter, we have started using a primitive method, which is by digging a hole in the ground, placing a metal tank, opening it, and so on.

There is no other solution or to wait a long time and a long line to use the bathroom, which is usually dirty due to the lack of anything and the large number of people

Ok. I thought so.

Sat, Feb 17 04:30 AM

05:10 AM

Sun, Feb 18 03:27 AM

How are you

04:11 AM

Hi Amira! Waiting to hear from you!!

Umm I'm fine not good but fine

Yes. I know

I hope this day will end very soon I'm very tired

Yes. I hear the news about Rafah.

I'm thinking about you and everyone there.

We need stop this war we want back to our life

Yes. I know. We want this for you.

We cannot imagine your suffering. We all want to help. Many people are still fighting for you every day.

04:52 AM

I am looking for words here. Amira, you have some more than any human should ever have to do. Every day I am looking for your communication. All the while knowing your suffering. None of us can know what you feel now. None of us can believe the cruelty of Israel. But we see it every day.

You have done more than any human should have to do.

I know that and I am proud that I am still steadfast and strong, but it is tiring sometimes, you know, in addition to the pain of war and missing Osama and his family, the problems that I suffer from here, and the great psychological pressure and the lack of respect for my feelings when my family receives that crazy person, it saddens me that they chose him. Many times, I thought about running away, traveling, or doing anything to get away, but All suggestions are difficult

Yes. They are. They seem impossible.

My son Roland put together a first draft of the book. There will be many changes and improvements to the layout. A lot of editing for me to do now. But I am sharing this first draft. I'll send it now.

Oh my thanks and gratitude to you and Roland. There will definitely be some editing to be better and very excited to see it

Yes. I'll send every draft. We still have to add the voice conversations.

You know, since we started talking about preparing this book, I have been thinking a lot about when I will be ready to say then that I have survived and will remain alive, and if the opposite happens and I do not live, but something remains after me and a story that the world knows.

Yes. Your story will live.

09:44 AM

Are all the quotes you put in your Facebook your original work?

Yes absolutely

Fantastic

Did you look at the rough first draft? We made it just to say we started 😊 😊

Yes I read all, it's fantastic

I am so glad you are pleased!!!!!

If there is anything you want taken out let me know. We will be adding the audio messages. Roland is doing that. He will also add the emojis.

OK I will and thanks very much for Roland 😊

Mon, Feb 19 12:48 PM

Amira. Tonight, in the small town of Athens, Ohio, where I am from, there is a city council meeting to vote on supporting a cease fire. My friend is going to read some of your writing at this meeting.

03:06 PM

Oh can you record that

I think the entire meeting will be recorded.

I asked her to record it. I also send the video of your home destruction.

04:06 PM

Tue, Feb 20 04:54 PM

Superstar

You are your very own brand of SUPERSTAR

Thanks

Yes. You're welcome.

Sat, Feb 24 01:59 PM

Are you there

Good evening

I heard there was bombing in Rafah

Yes I'm here how are you???

Maybe I let when reply that internet so bad

You are ok?

I am making sure

Audio: "It's true. Many bombings and explosions here in Rafah. But away from us. We can hear the noise, but we are not in danger. Thank you for your ask."

02:20 PM

Audio: "Okay, thank you for answering me. I saw the news, I just saw it and I wanted to check in on you to see how you were. Thinking about you every single day."

02:35 PM

[146] AMIRA ALZANEEN AND JEANNIE AMASH

Everything will be good

Yes

Amira, I am very sorry about what Osama is going through. I know this hurts you deeply.

Frankly, it is very, very difficult. For a while, they began to eat the food of animals and livestock there in the north, and now it is not available either, and other goods are expensive.

But trust God with them and He will not leave them

Audio: "Good evening, how are you today? I wish you are okay. Today I, um, don't know what to say, but I am tired, very tired. I'm now in the hospital in Rafah. My sister's husband had a gun in his leg. He will have operations. The situation is not very good. I hope everything will be okay."

Amira Amira. I am sorry. I am still here listening. I pray your brother-in-law is ok.

Photo 22D: a young man lying on a bed under a golden-brown floral-print blanket. His left calf is exposed, wrapped in white gauze and bloody bandages, with several metal rods supporting the injury.

I am grateful there is care for him. He looks strong. Where was he when he was shot

On the street near the school where they stay, he sells supplies to work and support his family

03:30 PM

A sniper. Thank God he is alive.

Yes Al Hamdallah

Yes

07:24 PM

I am very tired and afraid. We talked to Osama a little while ago. He is heading to the sea to get flour and food. I am very worried. He asks that we pray for him.

Hunger exhausted them, there was nothing to eat

Fri, Mar 01 07:08 AM

I am praying for him

09:11 AM

11:57 AM

Is Osama ok? Did he have success?

Audio: "Hi, how are you? Osama and his family are okay, he is very well. Thank God for everything. But for sorry he cannot get anything. No food, no aid, nothing. He come back from the north without anything, without flour, without eating . . . this is something we say very sorry for that, but Al Hamdallah for everything."

Fri, Mar 01 03:55 PM

Feeling Strange

A new month has begun, I sat thinking financially how these past five months have passed, what happened and how it happened, how we live a life that never resembled us before, away from our routines, our homes. We remain in tents on the streets, away from our cities and memories. How can we get used to this? How did all this pass? Nothing is as it once was. We share the same sleeping place, do everything together, even clothes and necessities, without complaint, no alternative. The things we used to do are no longer there. All our thoughts revolve around how to get food, drink, and stay safe. We've disconnected from everything, even from our feelings of sadness and shock, horror for every moment, but we don't know what to do, whether we know anything or not. We left our dreams behind, our simple wishes, our daily routines, and every nice feeling inside our hearts has been replaced with fear, terror, separation, and pain. Our current days are filled with exhaustion, hardship, and death. Nothing comes without a cost, but we paid the highest prices: catastrophe here, death there, hunger besieging every corner of this city except for destruction, explosions, and the absence of humanity. How? How did more than 150 days pass without notable change? We who loved life with all its ups and downs, but this is more than any human can bear or overcome. We will not surpass, we cannot. This is not humiliation; we are in the streets and houses, in every corner and alley, people scream, but there is no answer. Can't this war end? Hasn't what happened been enough, again? How have these days passed, where every second still slowly kills us, with no future occupying our minds, only to let the current day pass.

Amira Alzaneen Friday 1/3/2024

Sat, Mar 02 08:02 PM

Is it ok to put this photo in the book? Because it shows some of your hair

Sun, Mar 03 01:05 AM

No is not you know

05:42 AM

Ok. I thought this.

07:44 AM

You will have the book before we publish to give your opinion on everything. I am editing now. We will add up until the day.

08:07 AM

Audio: "That is good news, that is very good news. I will wait. Everything will be good, I'm sure about that."

Yes. It is wonderful

08:22 AM

08:40 AM

It is all your work from this time. Because you did it.

I will not be without you. Everything you do, it's great and big for me. Thank you

You are welcome.

Mon, Mar 04 01:37 PM

Hi Amira,

Photo 22A

Photo 22B

Photo 22C

Photo 22D

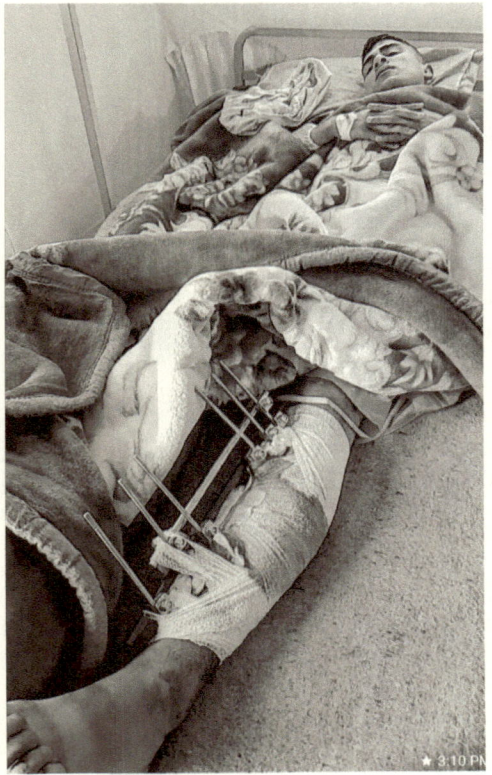

CHAPTER 23
MORE ACTS OF COURAGE

I don't know how language can be a form of social practice,
when we call a leave from death a "truce"

Wed, Mar 06 02:51 AM

I was thinking about do something

I have something on my mind that I would like to suggest to you. I mean, it came to me this morning after I spoke to my brother in the north, and my heart aches for the hunger they are going through at the moment, since Ramadan is near and people are leaving from the north to the south again due to extreme hunger. I have in mind the place separating Gaza and the south, the place they will first arrive at. There are people from Gaza. I should do something because they are coming here tired and exhausted, their health is weak, they are consumed by hunger, and they have walked very long distances, more than ten kilometers. I have in mind to prepare an envelope that contains simple things like two loaves of bread, a tomato, a cucumber, and a small bottle of water, and we go there to wait for them and offer it to them with the intention of our Lord, may God relieve it for us, them, and our Lord. It feeds all the hungry people, including my family and brothers, who are unable to reach their concerns

What is the way for this to happen? How can you find these supplies? How can I help?

Audio: "It's very easy. The supplies here we can buy it. The flour, the vegetables, the water. Everything we can find it here. After that we bring it to the way that they come from the north to the south. There we can walk together and give them the food, the water, help them as we can. You know that."

Audio: "Here we can work together, my mother and the girls. We can make the bread from the flour. We can make the vegetables with it and then maybe we can have a car to take us to there, and when the people they come from the north to here in the south and we give them the food, uh, help them to be strong, can hear what they have in this way, dangerous way. We look somehow to buy the supplies from the market or who can find it from here. You know everything we have here but it is a little expensive, but not very expensive."

I have something to tell you but I don't know how I can write about that

Today Osama's wife and her child Hassan come to the south. I go and bring them from the way between Gaza and Middle Gaza but for sorry

Osama still in the north

It was dangerous and the distance was very long. The street was blown up in the middle, separating Gaza from the center and the south. We walked a lot to reach before the checkpoint. There was destruction everywhere, deserted and scary. We had to be nearby and wait for them to arrive. It was very difficult until they arrived. Very scary. A long hug and crying. And the collapse. No one from my family knew that I had gone to get them. It was a surprise and a shock to everyone. We took some food, as I suggested to you, and water. They were hungry and very exhausted. The little Hassan ate three loaves of bread and many vegetables. Their condition was very sad. The worst thing was that Osama remained in the north. They fled from terror and hunger.

Video: the shadows of three people overlook a desolate scene of nothing, just dirt stretching to the sea, with a city in the distance.

Photo 23A.

Video: packages wrapped individually in plastic, like a piece of pita bread, a small cucumber, and a small tomato.

Photo 23B: the food packages of bread, cucumber, and tomato.

04:22 PM

Why did he stay?

Why did Osama stay?

Afraid of the risk that they would take him or kill him, as they did to many men

Oh my God. Yes, this is what I thought. He was saving his family. You went by yourself?

Yes, but it is forbidden to get too close. You must wait at a safe distance

You carried this food by yourself, and then hid, waiting for them? The courage for you to do this.

Yes, this is what happened. We made it to eat and baked it on the oven. I took some and bought some vegetables and water with what was left with me and distributed them to those who came from Gaza and the north. They were really hungry and lacked food.

Oh my God Amira. You are brave. Your love conquered your fear.

This is natural and our instinct. You know what is strange about the matter is that at that time I thought, if they did not arrive, I would continue on my way and return to Gaza and the north, and what would happen would happen.

I believe you would have done this. You would have walked all the way to your brother.

I believe you still want to.

I'm sorry he is not there.

Exactly I miss him so much and afraid 👥🤍

Yes.

Sat, Mar 09 12:08 PM

How old are Yusef and Mohammad??

Mohammad

Yusef.

Muhammad is the way you spell it, yes?

Yes exactly 💯

How old are they?

Mohammad, 12 years old, Yusef, 10 year, born February 29, at four years come one time.

Leap year baby! My best friend from when I was in High School, she is a leap year baby!

Oh

How old is Jorey?

5 years old

Thanks.

Tue, Mar 12 09:13 AM

First aid ship to Gaza leaves Cyprus port in pilot project

http://www.theguardian.com/world/2024/mar/12

They will be landing in the North.

11:26 AM

Praying.

01:29 PM

Have you seen our beautiful moons?

Have you seen the angel, my cousins?

This is Batoul, her mother's beloved.

By the way, she has twins, only six months old. They grew up in war.

By the way, yesterday my aunt and her moons went to God. The house was bombed over their heads, without warning. Batoul was in her mother's arms. They found her, and to this day, Lin has not been seen. They are searching for her under the rubble.

That was better for them than remaining in this ugly world.

Paradise is fitting for them, and they are the most beautiful birds in paradise

07:40 PM

I'm very tired

I cannot describe my feeling and the great fatigue. It is exhausting. I received heartbreaking news that stopped my heart. My youngest aunt and her twin girls, who were only 6 months old, have passed away. They blew up the house, hitting their heads. They killed them. They are all gone, little angels who did nothing unharmed in the house. In cold blood, they were killed.

08:46 PM

Amira. They are truly angels now.

They didn't deserve this death. No one can justify this.

Wed, Mar 13 07:10 AM

Photo 23C: a beautiful six-month-old baby girl, Batul, with large, clear, blue eyes.

Photo 23D: same Batul, wrapped in a blanket, clearly deceased.

10:41 AM

This is unbearable. I'm sorry. I'm so very sorry.

11:03 AM

Please tell me their names. Did your Aunt survive?

11:19 AM

She doesn't. She die. And the two girls, we find Batul, until now we cannot find Lin. It's miss...we miss her. They are still looking about her in the home destroyed.

11:50 AM

I'm sorry. Oh Amira, I know your heart is heavy.

06:27 PM

Photo 23E: Lin.

Photo 23F: Amira cradling Batul's body wrapped in a bloody shroud.

Photo 23A

Photo 23B

Photo 23C

Photo 23D

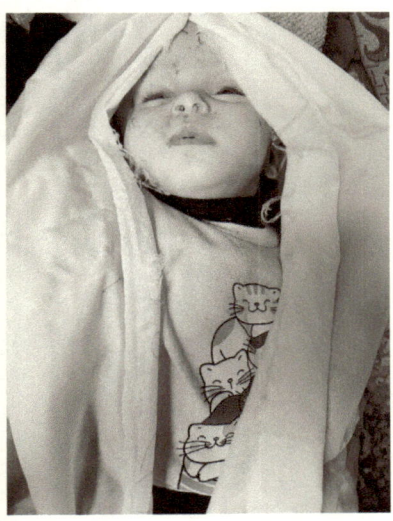

Photo 23E

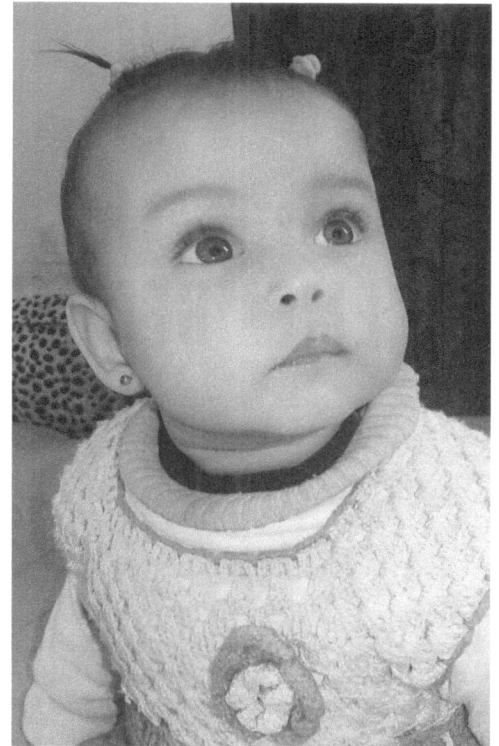

Photo 23F

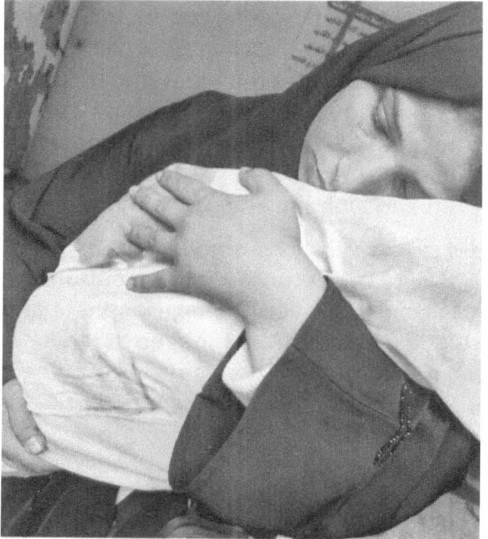

CHAPTER 24
SO REMEMBER ME

I fear that we will spend our lives imagining things,
hoping they will happen and they will not.

Thu, March 21 11:05 AM

It's not the end yet. After more than 165 years of this fierce war in Gaza, it continues. We had hoped everything would end before the blessed month of Ramadan, but today is the eleventh day of Ramadan, and it hasn't stopped. There's no respect for the holy month. We fast from hunger due to the lack of food and the blockade. Even as the fasting month approaches, we pray and invoke Allah to end everything soon.

The number of casualties has exceeded 35,000, with 75,000 wounded and many more missing. Over 90% of Gaza is now rubble and destruction, resembling a ghost town. Famine in the north, soaring prices, and overcrowding in the south. We think daily about when we'll return to our homes and peaceful lives, but instead, massacres, genocide, cold-blooded killings of children and women, and much more continue.

These days are terrifying, resembling the beginning of the war. Israeli brutality has returned, with occupation forces and indiscriminate bombing everywhere. Hospitals and residential areas are being invaded, and houses demolished over the heads of their inhabitants. There's no safe place, no peace. The nights are terrifying, and every sunrise brings the sound of reconnaissance aircraft and very annoying F-16s, like a psychological war killing us slowly.

When we move away, yes, we die here every day, more than a thousand times, just to get food and safety. We can't afford to grieve or weaken; we resist with all our strength to remain steadfast. Getting out of this city is harder than living in it. It's not the end, but I've decided there must be a conclusion. Our days are all filled with death. I fear becoming just another number, another statistic, another lost soul. But my current dream, my foremost thought, is for the world to know what we're living through, what we're suffering.

We don't want to be anonymous stories; we want the world to know our painful tale and to stop these wars that erase human existence from the world record in a terrible and final way, without any trial for these crimes. For everyone reading this, I know your mind couldn't have imagined that we've experienced all of this, and if tears fall, I congratulate you. It proves the greatness and beauty of the emotions you have, your fear for any human soul and your belief in its right to life, dreams, and wishes. Be in my place and imagine the magnitude and horror of the tragedy I'm trying to describe as best I can, yet it's still not enough. What's happening is catastrophic and unimaginable.

This is my message; this is my cause. If I departed and have passed away, tell it to the whole world and to those you know. We are here now, but at any moment, we might not be.

By the way, I'd like to inform you that our hearts have grown cold, and we've lost the sanctity of our days. There's no time to live, no time to cry, no passion for tomorrow, no hope for salvation. Our survival this time may not happen next time.

Don't leave us alone.

From the city abandoned by all, where they kill everything in it every moment, and they turn their backs on it, ignoring it. Here is Gaza, fighting to survive.

It might be the end of my life, not just the end of this book. So always remember Amira.

Amira Alzaneen

Phoenix Gaza

Special note from Jeannie: At first, we were going to end the book here. But the war has continued fiercely, and there are more stories to tell. We extended the timeline to include the beginning of August. We continue to rally, support, and believe in the possibility of peace and justice for all peoples.

PART 2

CHAPTER 25
CARRYING ON

And do not make my companionship a misfortune, nor my presence a burden, nor my speech a harm, my Lord, make me light in the passage, the rest of the trace, and to be blessed with good fortune, content, happy and flourishing wherever I am, O God

Thu, March 23 10:19 PM

I was watching a video a while ago that hurt my heart a lot and made me cry. It is disastrous. They enjoy killing innocent people as if they are playing.

It is impossible for a normal person to understand this.

10:51 PM

Video from Amira: A young man walks down a dirt road, is shot, and begins crawling—then he is blown up in a cloud of smoke. This repeats for another young man, then a group of four young men. All are left dead in the dirt. A sad song in Arabic plays. This is not a video taken by Amira, but one taken by an unknown civilian in Gaza and shared throughout.

Photos 25A, 25B, 25C, 25D, 25E, 25F, 25G.

Sat, Mar 23 09:34 PM

It is a very terrible and catastrophic matter. There is a crime, according to what witnesses say, that army soldiers stormed one of the houses near Al-Shifa Hospital and brutally beat everyone in it. A woman begged them not to beat her, as she was in her fifth month of pregnancy, but after she cried, they dragged her and forced her to take off her clothes in front of the men, her husband, and his brothers. Then they assaulted and raped her in front of them, and shot anyone who closed their eyes and did not see this atrocity. Then, after they exhausted her one by one, they shot her in the feet, expelled her from the outside, and displaced the family to the south, and no one knew anything about her until this moment. Was she dead or what happened? I cannot imagine. Such a huge violation

10:25 PM

God. I can't even imagine. Please do not think about it Amira. It is the worst, most evil of human behavior.

Sun, March 24 05:01 AM

I was unable to respond properly. I couldn't take it in. We are truly witnessing evil running wild in the global stage, reported on all social media, yet governments, mine, are allowing it. May God forgive them. History will never forget this. Gaza will go on the right side of it. Your words will help show this.

I hope

05:27 AM

Me too.

You are in my thoughts and prayers today, Amira.

08:23 AM

Thanks for everything

08:54 AM

Always.

How are you today

9:51 AM

Try to be fine

10:03 AM

What about you

10:32 AM

Hi Amira, I am out walking with my roommate's dog. Her name is Sally. I am ok. I am living in a different world than you. Even when I ask you 'How are you', it's difficult to even ask you that because I know, your world, right now, is not an easy one. But I'm thinking about you and I'll send you a picture of the dog.

10:48 AM

Audio: "Hello, how are you? You make me smile with this post. I wish for you a good and happy time. It's a beautiful name, Sally. I wish everything will be good, everything will be fine. One day I will tell you I will be very very good. When this war will end, we will come back for our homes. The situation will be better, the bombings stop. And as you listen, I sit with my family [there are children's voices in the background], they are [giggles] screaming. I wish for you a good day."

Thu, March 28 06:11 AM

Hi Amira. I am thinking about you and praying for you

I'm trying to be fine but this difficult 😔 🙃

I am hearing the news. It is catastrophic.[5]

Heartbreaking.

We have nothing

06:50 AM

Amira, are there any aid trucks getting in at all?

Audio: "Yes, absolutely we have some, but hard to get it, you know. The prices, it's very expensive and now it's Ramadan, Al Hamdallah for everything, but we are trying to be good. Trying to be safety, trying to be okay. [Deep sigh.] For how long I don't know how we will stay like that."

---

5 On March 28, 2024, Al Jazeera reported that, according to the United Nations Office for the Coordination of Humanitarian Affairs, Israel had murdered nearly 160 people and injured nearly 200 during the last two days. It also reported that nearly two-thirds of the hospitals had been rendered nonfunctional, with many others being minimally functional. Most of the deaths were in northern Gaza City.

Photo 25A

Photo 25B

Photo 25C

Photo 25D

لا يمكن وصف كمية الظلم الذي يحدث لنا 💔

Photo 25E

لا يمكن وصف كمية الظلم الذي يحدث لنا 💔

Photo 25F

لا يمكن وصف كمية الظلم الذي يحدث لنا 💔

Photo 25G

لا يمكن وصف كمية الظلم الذي يحدث لنا 💔

CHAPTER 26
IMAGINING SCENES OF RETURN

Gratitude lifts you up and lifts you out of the cycle of injustice,
oppression, and comparison. Whenever you feel hopeless, take
a minute and force yourself to count your blessings—one, two,
three—until your heart is purified, your energy is renewed, and the
darkness and despair are completely removed. Gratitude increases
sustenance, opens the mind, broadens the heart, and opens paths.
Praise be to God, the Rich, the Most Generous. Praise be to God,
Lord of the Worlds, until He is pleased.

Imagining Scenes of Return

Hundreds of thousands rush, racing against the wind, returning to their haven, their homes. Their memories, details, and safety await. Hugs filled with longing and eagerness for those distances parted by horror and fear, prevented from meeting due to complete severance. Tears flow, hearts break, witnessing the magnitude of destruction and ash left by this brutal war.

The city stands empty, akin to a ghost town, terrifying in every corner. Each corner holds a story, a victim, a massacre, a humanitarian disaster. This is what this war has left behind: crimes, genocide, and no solace to console every loss, every missing person, every grieving and wounded soul.

Everything starts from scratch, and even if there's a new beginning, these days won't be easily surpassed. The scenes won't leave our minds; we're completely extinguished, trying to lie to ourselves as much as we can that everything will be alright. But it remains a lie, deceiving ourselves. No one is spared from pain in all its forms.

Perhaps gradually, life will return as it did during the war days, but it's incredibly exhausting, far from easy. We need decades for life to return to normal, and even if it does, it won't be the same. This story will remain etched inside us, a bleeding wound whenever we remember it.

Yet, how we wish for a swift return to our lives, our homes, our tranquility, our basic rights to live. The scenes of return will be greater than this by far. No one can continue and adapt to living another life elsewhere, under different circumstances, as we do now. Let these days pass quickly, for they have become exceedingly heavy and painful.

Amira Alzaneen

04:29 PM

You are wonderful and smart and a budding brilliant writer who expresses herself in a way that touches people immediately.

This is the heart of the book.

Yes, that's why I don't worry at all if something happens to me. I will survive with this book.

Sun, March 31 07:21 PM

Photo 26A: a woman cradling a wrapped dead child with blood on the sheet.

Who is this woman?

08:50 PM

It's me and my aunt's child

9:08 PM

Ok. I thought so. I wanted to be sure. I am sorry Amira. So very sorry.

I think I didn't want to believe you had this pain.

Al Hamdallah for everything

09:37 PM

Photo 26A

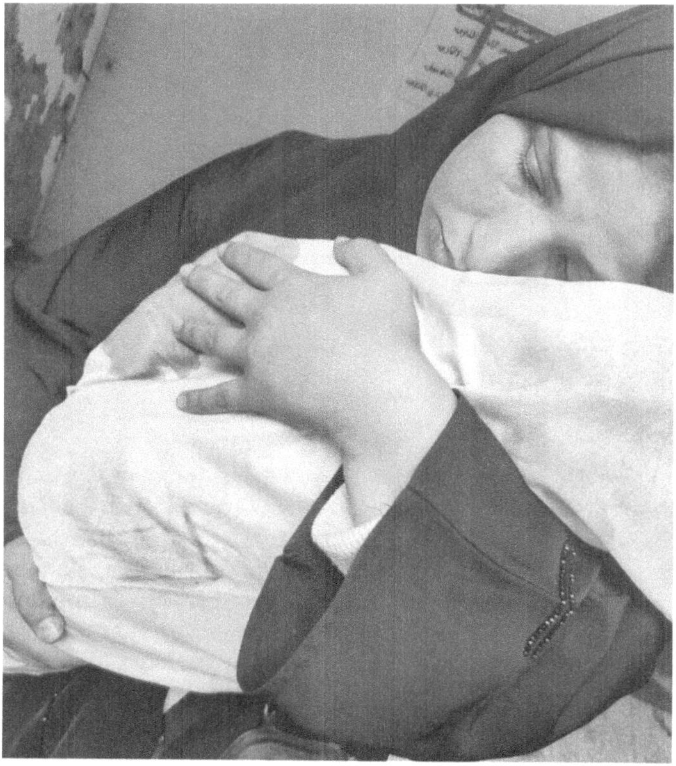

CHAPTER 27
PRIMITIVE LIFE

The heart is in pain and the soul cries, and the separation and loss have been prolonged. Eid comes and goes, and the sadness remains the same, and the feelings of pain over the loss of loved ones do not go away. How I wished that we could rejoice on Eid with the closeness of loved ones, but they left and left the pain, an eternal Eid, lost, missing, and displaced. Your Eid in heaven is sweeter, my dearest beloved, my aunt and her moon, my uncle, my cousins, companions, loved ones, colleagues, and many others. We have no Eid without them, and they bring us together and reunite with the dearest of my soul, my brother, my uncles, their children, and many others in the north. Happy New Year

Tue, April 2

Primitive Life

Primitive life is what we have been living for over 6 months without electricity, water, or even a source of food. We live in tents, using fire to cook food and prepare our daily needs. Our days pass by fulfilling daily tasks like fetching water, cleaning, organizing, and other strenuous tasks that we never imagined doing in this manner. We suffer from extreme heat during the day and biting cold at night. It's a life unlike ours, in a place unfamiliar to us. The idea of bathing once or twice a week and living without internet or connection, even waiting in line to use the bathroom, is not pleasant at all. Moreover, waiting

in long lines for bread and essential supplies, everything requires enduring long waits, if you're lucky enough to get your
share. The unusual congestion in the streets requires more
than an hour to travel a ten-minute journey. We wash one set
of clothes and wear the other, and so on. You're fortunate if
you have a source of power, a bathroom to use, and abun-
dant water, or even more fortunate if you have gas, some cold
water, and your own bed. Your happiness is finding a car to go
somewhere, and many details that were not of great impor-
tance in our lives before the war, we didn't miss them. Houses have been replaced by tents, and the old alternatives are
now what we use to spend our days and ease their difficulty.
What's available is better than what's not.

Amira Alzaneen

Thu, April 4 03:52 AM

Hi Amira, you are in my thoughts and heart every day. I don't
know why God allows this; I cannot ever understand the evil
playing on planet Earth. I know that you are pushed to the ex-
tremes of your tolerance as a woman, in every way. I love you
dearly. No matter what, your courage and love are a beacon to us
all. I'm praying for you. I am thankful for you. I'm sorry for the
cruel world that has twisted itself in the wrong direction. There
are many people still trying to help the situation, but I know it
may not reach you. Try to find one small piece of beauty today.
And when you do, please tell me what you found.

Dear beautiful and beloved Jeannie, I appreciate your words
and you are always in my prayers and thoughts. I trust God
very much, and will be fine and better. One day everything
that is bad will change to become beautiful in one moment,
and if that is delayed, I am forced to remain strong to fight.
I will continue with everything I wish for and achieve my
dreams that are lost every day. The situation I will not hide
from you is difficult and miserable and I do not have anything. However, I try to hold on to hope and patience and
make something beautiful for every day. Yesterday I prepared

breakfast for them. Today we will prepare sweets and distribute them to people as a mercy to the souls of our dead. My uncle and aunt do not have anything. Something, but we try to make something with what exists. God has destined this and God is responsible for it.

Much love always to you and all of you.

You are always doing the best thing. Your incredible spirit is an inspiration for us all.

04:30 AM

04:49 AM

Audio: "I know. I know what I'm sure about it is I'm strong and I will stay strong. I have a dream. I have a HOPE for tomorrow if I have tomorrow to live, if I have a life to continue. I am sure that I want to be a successful woman, to prove to everyone that I can do the most beautiful thing. The most perfect thing. You know that. I want to prove to everyone that I can do everything by myself."

Mon, April 8 09:26 PM

I am tired, thinking about the Eid that will be on Wednesday, how we will spend it, what we will do, and how we will provide for the children's needs.

09:40 PM

What do you need?

Are aid trucks coming in?

It come everyday but not for everyone

Summer is approaching, the temperatures have risen, they need clothes, even I am tired, we were not like this

Can you buy clothes?

Everything is available here, but the war merchants sell the most. Even the aid is sold. I do not have the price for some of what I need.

All the aid is sold? By the people driving the trucks?

Not all, some yes for sorry and what comes not enough

Tell me what you can do. I can have a little fundraiser with my family.

We can search for long hours by wandering around the market until we get the clothes and supplies we need at the lowest prices, not cheap, but less expensive than others.

Tue, April 9 08:44 AM

Tomorrow is the first day of Eid and the vacation begins

Wed, April 10 08:58 AM

We are putting together a family donation.

09:09 AM

Audio: *"Good evening how are you? I wish you are okay. For you from us I wish Happy Eid. I wish this war end very soon. Thank you for your family, thank you for everyone who help with you, everyone who supports us. Thanks for everything."*

09:31 AM

Thu, April 11 07:48 AM

Hi Amira, Happy Eid. I know it's a little bit late but people are giving money and I will be able to send you either by this afternoon or tomorrow. Everyone is thinking about you and hoping that it helps.

I will be back in touch and I will send as soon as I have it all. Four families from my son's wife's family have pledged to give.

11:41 AM

Audio: *"Good evening and how are you and happy Eid for EVERY ONE in this world. After that I want to thank you and thank all families that support us and help us . . . I know that you are thinking of me all the time, and I want you to thank the family, all the family, and tell them all my love for them and all my prayers. I don't know what to do and what to say, but this is a big thing for me—that when I think somebody is thinking of me, still remembering me, that is a big thing for me. You know. My word is not enough for me to prove that it is a big thing. We hope that the situation will be different the next day. We don't know [if] there will be dangers . . . be safety . . . We will wait. May God help us, may God [be] with us, may this war end very soon. This is all what we want, all what we wish. [Small laugh.] We are very tired, you know."*

Audio: *"And I will send for you a recording that I hope you will send for the family who help me, to thank them, they thinking of me is a big thing, support [for] me is important and I respect everything that they do for me. And the little thing I can do for them is I want to thank them."*

Audio: *"Hi there, how are you? I am Amira from Gaza. Most of you know me from my friend Jeannie, or from my writing on Facebook or social media. I just want to thank everyone for everything they do for us. Thinking of us, supporting us, helping us. Everything you do is a big thing that makes a difference in my heart. Feel me that I'm very happy to know people like you, thinking of us, and I respect everything that you do. I hope that war will end very soon. Maybe someday we can see each other, talking, I don't know, or happen a good thing . . . the little thing that I can give for you that I'm really really from my heart, all love for you, all respect. I just want that maybe in the future, I have a good future, have a happy life, and this war will end. What you do, even if it was a little but it is very very big. Maybe my words are not enough to tell you how much I am happy to know people like you. I'm proud, I'm very proud. Thank you for everything. From my heart, thanks, and hope that for all the time you will be okay. I hope that this war has many people like you who love, help us and thinking of us and support us. All my love for you.*

"At the end I have one message for you. I just want to tell you that, don't give up. Don't give up any day to do anything even if it is little. You don't know, maybe that thing that was a little made a big change in this world. Continue. Continue and do what you can."

Fri, April 12 08:38 AM

I think the family would love photos of the children when they receive some of their clothes. This made them happy to give.

Absolutely

Sun April 14, 04:48 AM

Audio: "The news about coming back to the north. Some families this morning trying to go back, on Rashid Street by the sea. Come back from the south to the north. Now many families try to go for their homes. I don't know, maybe I can go to see Osama, taking the family to the north; I'm still waiting to be sure it is the right thing, to be sure we can go."

06:01 AM

Audio: "Please keep telling me what you are doing. Thank you for telling me. It's . . . boy . . . you are living in times that are so uncertain, and every decision that you make has a huge impact. I will be looking for your messages."

06:56 AM

Audio: "If you go to the north, will you go by yourself? Or who will accompany you?"

Audio: *"I am still waiting here in Rafah. I cannot go back for the north; the way is not safety. The bombing and explosions there have the people there who come back from the north, the situation is very dangerous. We cannot decide to come back now. We hope, we hope, that everything will be ok."*

07:27 AM

Audio: *"We don't know. My sister and her husband come back, but they still on the street for now. We don't know; the explosion and bombing has many people injured and dead. They kill the people who come back from the north. I will try to contact them to come back here. I am still in Rafah, I don't think I can come back for the moment for the north. The situation is still very dangerous."*

07:49 AM

Instagram post sent by Jeannie about Columbia University students.[6]

The world is exploding.

01:05 PM

I want to tell you the money has arrived here in Rafah and we will have it in the morning.

03:11 PM

---

6 Columbia University began some of the very first on-campus protests against the genocide in Gaza. The official start date of the encampment on the campus was April 17, 2024. Participants pitched fifty tents and called it the Gaza Solidarity Encampment. Although the university president (who was later forced to resign), Minouche Shafik, authorized the NYPD to conduct mass arrests during this peaceful protest, the participants rebuilt the encampment the next day. Lasting more than one month and two weeks, the Columbia University Student Encampment went on to inspire national and international encampments, with over 140 colleges and universities across the USA, and 247 globally. (Palestineiseverywhere.com)

Love you. Proud of you.

Me to so much

Thank you.

CHAPTER 28
WHAT IS HOMELAND?

Do you think after all this, Gaza will rise from the rubble?

Mon, April 15

It's more than just family, home, friends, neighbors, streets, and district; it's the places you love, the corner where you find peace, filled with memories and details, your joy and pain, your failures and successes, your weakness and strength, your laughter and tears!!!

For those left in Gaza, it's become like any other place... just land like any other land... the spirit within it has died... the homeland within it has vanished... the passion has been lost... dreams have been buried... all turned into rubble and ashes... life without the scent of life... and still, we haven't fully grasped what happened!!!

In the past, our elders taught us that manhood doesn't quarrel when you have your family with you or when you're at home, so you don't dishonor your family and expose them to danger. The family is the victim, and not even a home, a street, a friend, a neighbor, or the details of our lives remain in history!!!

Today marks the 192nd day of death.

Tue, April 16 9:32 AM

Did you receive the funds?

10:18 AM

Yes today I have it

Great!!

Wed, April 17 02:30 AM

Audio: "Good evening dear. How are you? I wish you are okay, in good health, and have a good day. I get the money. I buy something for Hassan and his mother, Osama's wife. They come from the north, they here now."

04:26 AM

Photos 28A, 28B, 28C, 28D, and 28E: the children and their new clothes. Two photos of children playing in the water on the beach at sunset. A photo of Hassan, her nephew, leaning into her on her lap, eyes closed.

Thu, April 18 06:31 AM

Is this Hassan?

Yes

He loves you.

Yes, so much

Amira and I had a rare opportunity to video chat for three minutes. I was able to see her living conditions, the family, and the children. Living in a world of endless tents with no amenities, very little privacy, they were all smiling in their new clothes. Even living in makeshift tents in the sweltering heat, they were all playing in this moment, laughing and grateful.

Audio: "I'm very happy to see you and to see the friends that are there. The internet is not very well, I cannot see you very good. Yes, this is Hassan. I buy the clothes for him yesterday and some for his mother. Will call you when the internet will be good. I will make coffee for now. I am really very very happy to see you."

Sat, April 20 10:10 PM

Audio: The persistent buzz of an Israeli drone overhead. The audio continues for forty-eight seconds.

I am praying for all of you.

Sun, April 21 06:05 AM

Are you there Amira?

06:25 AM

I'm here but I'm very tired

06:46 AM

Yes. I am sure you did not sleep. Thankful you are there

10:08 AM

Note: Amira had been struggling in a short-lived, dysfunctional marriage. Her now ex-husband had caused trouble numerous times for her. I have left these incidents out, mostly for her privacy, and because she has expressed a desire to write about this in the broader context of Arab society later. However, here we share the good news of her divorce.

Wed, April 24 09:07 AM

I got divorce today

I'm free

10:49 AM

Audio: "Hooray! I am so happy to hear this. Oh man, I smiled when I read this."

11:31 AM

It was not a simple matter, and his bad deeds increased. He blackmailed me, and I increased the amount of money that I paid him to complete this divorce. It does not matter. I bought my freedom.

11:47 AM

Thank God.

12:08 PM

For everything

Yes.

12:30 PM

I'm going to write something titled I Bought My Freedom

Photo 28A

Photo 28B

Photo 28C

Photo 28D

CHAPTER 29
I HAVE BOUGHT MY FREEDOM

Not all harm is obvious, and not every harmful person has it written on his forehead that he is harmful. Poisonous words are harmful, lack of appreciation is harmful, underestimating the sadness of others is harmful, lying is harmful. Harm has many forms and its effects are not necessarily seen on the features of the person in front of us.

For a moment, some might think this is just a joke or a jest, perhaps fodder for mockery. But there is nothing strange about it. I paid some cash for my release, my salvation from a failed relationship that only caused me pain and complete weakness. I am no longer the person who negotiates with another for their freedom and peace. A man who doesn't gamble to keep a woman. But it's okay. I was living through a period akin to death, without ending this relationship. And if its end came with paying money, that's fine. It's more evidence that it shouldn't continue in any form. Cutting it off is the best. There was a great pressure on my heart, and today I felt immense relief. Nothing will weaken me; I will remain strong always. It's enough that I held onto my decision and wasn't coerced into anything I strongly reject. I am very happy and consider it a great achievement. I have become free, independent in myself. It's time to think about my constructive future, my goals, and chase my dreams and aspirations. I will overcome, days will pass, and everything will get better. All that is bad will go, and the beautiful will come. I have great faith in this.

Fight hard to succeed.

24/4/2024, a special date for a more special day.

The first day of freedom.

Amira Alzaneen

Mon, April 29 03:55 PM

Thank you. You did very well.

I was wish it was before more than that

05:26 PM

It was amazing and I am glad you did it

05:46 PM

Fri, May 3 06:49 AM

Hi there how are you

Hey. Been waiting to hear from you.

I'm fine with to have a good news we hope

Me too. We hope so.

08:45 AM

Are you still able to receive funds?

Yes, like last time, this is possible

Ok. Thank you. GoFundMe is asking many questions.

Ok

12:24 PM

What is your mother's name? GoFundMe wants names of other adults who may benefit.

12:57 PM

And father's name

02:09 PM

My mother is Siham and my father is Abed

Thank you.

So welcome

Waiting for being able to send.

02:22 PM

OK we will see

But I try to open the link I can't

For GoFundMe?

Yes

I don't know why that is....

Can you send it for me

02:46 PM

Seem things can't open it

It is working for me. I wonder if it is your connection.

I don't know

It's ok.

I am working on it

Good

CHAPTER 30
ISRAEL'S LIE OF RAFAH

I don't know how language can be a form of social practice,
when we call a leave from death a "truce"?

Mon, May 6 05:08 AM

I am afraid, and at the same time I do not feel anything or think. The news is bad. They informed some areas in Rafah to evacuate, and this is very scary. The explosions are getting closer every day, but I no longer care because what happens, happens. We live in fear. I do not know what kind of life this is.

06:56 AM

Audio: "Hi Amira. Reading your message, and yes, I have been aware of this for quite a while. There is a big debate on the news about Israel invading Rafah, and people are still protesting about it. But . . . Israel will do what Israel will do. And unfortunately, we don't know what they will do. Israel has made it very clear that it does not care about the hostages. I don't know if you hear this, but many people in Israel are protesting against Netanyahu. There's just so much bad at play right now. I think about you a lot. We are praying for your safety. Let me know if funds are still available. GoFundMe is being very difficult about getting funds to Palestine. I'm sorry about that. They're asking a lot of questions, so just keep me informed and let me know what's happening. [Deep sigh.] I'm sorry, I'm angry. I'm also hoping and praying, all these things at once for you. And I understand how it is very difficult to feel because there are too many feelings. Too many for a person to have to endure. I hope that all the little children will gather around you when you put your arms around them. I feel that you are one of their saviors. I feel that those children need you. Stay with them. I love you very much, and stay in touch as well as you can."

07:06 AM

OK I will hope everything be good

03:31 PM

There is some good news that we really hope will continue and everything will end

03:42 PM

What is the good news??

There is approval by the Palestinian side of the truce and cease-fire agreement, and they are awaiting the Israelis' response

This is good news.

Yes

We are waiting

Yes.

05:31 PM

Praying for you.

08:17 PM

Stay in touch. Communicate if you can.[7]

Tue, May 7 01:20 AM

Bad news. It was a difficult night for Rafah, and now occupation tanks are present at the Rafah travel crossing.

Video: Israeli army tank approaching the Rafah border, lowering its guns. This video was taken from someone inside the tank, so it is an Israeli video.

07:12 AM

You are alive. The main thing

08:22 AM

Are you in the east of Rafah

No, we are now in west of Rafah

Ok.

Wed, May 8 05:31 AM

Hi dear Amira. Are you there

Hi yes, I'm here

I'm thinking about you.

But to be honest, I am tired and I fear that I will become de-

---

7 On May 6, 2024, Hamas agreed to a three-stage ceasefire proposal that was put forth by Egypt and Qatar. Israel did not agree, and continued to bomb and assault civilians in Gaza. In fact, Israel seized the Rafah Egyptian border on May 7. The full proposed agreement can be viewed on the Al Jazeera website, https://www.aljazeera.com/news/2024/5/6/text-of-the-ceasefire-proposal-approved-by-hamas.

pressed. Two days ago, I was tired of thinking about what is happening. I tried a lot to write, but the description makes me tired. It is too much to bear and anticipating what will happen is very bad. The conditions are very difficult and the sounds are approaching like the beginning of the war.

I think that the pressure is enormous. No one can imagine your stress.

I understand the tired feelings. You weren't designed to live like that. How are the children?

CHAPTER 31
A NEW NIGHTMARE

A person progresses to the extent that he motivates others to progress, and is provided for to the extent that he is a source of their provision. Blessings shower him when he is a key to goodness, and happiness knocks on the doors of his heart when he is not stingy with it for others. This is because in life there is a law of loyalty: whoever gives sincerely will be answered.

It's not new, but a nightmare that has been haunting me for over six months since the day we fled from northern Gaza to the south in search of some safety, away from the explosions and southern massacres, the nightmare of war that could reach this place we thought would remain safe. But instead, occupation arrived, explosions everywhere, children killed, homes destroyed, and genocide. The same scenes repeating themselves once again, people fleeing aimlessly, just to stay alive, crowdedness, skyrocketing prices, the sound of gunfire, tank attacks. Unfortunately, Rafah crossing was occupied, controlled by the enemy, with their fire belts, smoke, and ash filling the air. Sad and fearful faces, tears filling the eyes, terrifying nights. I no longer know how long this will last, my heart pounding with fear, my face paler. We have no energy left; it's been too long, death approaching with every moment. There's nothing to do; we're all alone, mere truces and false agreements that changed nothing. No one cared about the bloodshed, destruction, and killing. The earth's solutions have ended; everything is left to the sky now.

Only God is capable of everything.

Amira Alzaneen

05:44 AM

Afraid nothing to do

If there is any comfort at all in knowing that people here are caring about you. We are stunned at the actions of our government. We are still standing up. If it helps at all. Every day I am thinking about you. My heart is also heavy. Grateful I know you even though I am watching the world be crazy.

We hope everything ends and come back to our life

06:18 AM

Everything will end, I hope. Exiting Gaza was difficult because of its cost, but staying safe is now impossible because of their presence at the crossing.

Yes. I heard about that.

04:04 PM

Audio of Israeli drones flying overhead, loud and close.

Stay close to your brothers and sisters.

Very bad noise. We are together

05:42 PM

Good

Thu, May 9 12:32 PM

Hi Amira. I am following the news and social media about Rafah. Are you still in your same place?

Audio: "Hello good evening how are you? Yes, we are still staying here in the west of Rafah. The situation now is good, everything is away from us. We wait. We will see what will happen. We hope everything will end very soon."

God Bless you Amira. I think about you a lot.

Fri, May 10 09:07 AM

Hi Amira. Checking on you today.

01:42 PM

Good the weather very hot

02:59 PM

The heat! Do you have water?

Are you still able to receive funds?

Audio: "Yes, we are still in our place, we don't move anywhere. We don't know what the situation will be in the day. The situation is different. Not the same. We don't know what will be happening, but we hope it will end, but when we cannot, I don't know what to say, imagine the end of this war. Yes, of course I can [receive funds]. The bombing, explosions everywhere but away from us. Some people go for another place, they take their tent, they take their things and move around, away. I don't know what to say, but I feel very tired. I feel that unless everything will be different, everything is hard. The internet connection is so bad. The man we take connection from, he want to move around to another place. He took out all the server internet from here. We don't know what to do.

"The water for now we have, but after that we don't know. Many cars, many trucks, many things, the people arrive from many places like Khan Younis, Deir al-Balah, Maghazi, middle Gaza. They don't know where they go, they don't know what

to do. They haven't anything. They still arrive and arrive as refugees looking for a safe place away from the bombing. The situation is very sad. I feel that I want to cry, but I can't."

Sat, May 11 04:09 AM

Audio: "Dear, good morning, how are you? I wish you are okay. I know the time is different between us, many hours. The situation today is different from the last day, but they ask from the people still in the north in Gaza to go out for West Gaza, and here in Rafah has many refugees, asking them to go for Khan Younis. They are away from us, but we don't know what will happen."

12:07 PM

Video: Young boy walking across an empty yellow-brown area of dirt. Down the road, we see the remaining tents.

Photos 31A, 31B, 31C.

Your video?

Yes

This place was crowded with tents and people and now it is not crowded, everyone is running away and moving. Scared, they don't know where to go. It's really tiring

You are staying. I understand that there is no decision. Because there are no answers.

I want to cry, but I can't. Even in the north, it's bad. The war has started again, and there's bombing everywhere

Exactly. There is no safe place, transportation is expensive, and the search for water, food, and life again in an unknown place

There is no way to cry. There is too much to feel. We end up feeling nothing. Until much later. It is how to survive

Photo 31D: women sitting in a group outside of their tent cluster.

Photo 31E: Amira, her eyes full of the sadness and despair she feels.

This is what happens, but we have no energy. Everything is extinguished. We try to survive with our bodies and souls, but from within us we are slowly dying.

01:15 PM

Two videos: trucks and cars packed with belongings amongst the crowds of people fleeing again.

Photos 31F, 31G.

You are alive. In one of the most difficult situations in the entire world.

I struggle to find words to tell you. You matter and you are important.

So happy to have person like you

01:53 PM

Very lucky

04:16 PM

You matter and I am the lucky one too!

Sun, May 12 01:14 AM

Mon, May 13 08:23 AM

Audio: "Hi dear, good evening. How are you? I wish you are okay today. For sorry, the contact of the internet, the place where we are stay in it, turned off. We don't have any internet. I walked for a whole [unclear] to have, to send this message for you. We are okay. We still in Rafah. We don't think to go for anywhere at the moment. We don't know what will happen, but we hope that everything will be okay. I will tell you everything time and time and send messages. Don't worry, we are very good. I will send a picture for you for me and Jorie, when we can use the internet and send it for you."

Photo 31H: Amira and Jorie, her sister. Jorie is wearing a red, white and blue tie-dye shirt.

Video with audio: "All that stayed here in the tent—now the place is so empty. Everyone traveling for another place, looking for some safety. I don't know, Rafah is not dangerous as they say, but they are scared from the bombings, explosions, strikes. They going away, and we still here."

08:53 AM

Audio: "Hi Amira, I'm sending you money. Please let me know you can still receive it this way. As soon as I hear from you, I'm going to send it. Let me know! Thank you."

11:10 AM

Audio: "Yes, absolutely, I can still receive it. I will try to be in contact on the internet to know everything. Thank you, thank you so much."

Tue, May 14 10:20 AM

Audio: "Good morning, how are you? I wish you are okay. The internet contact, it come back but it is not very good, but a little from time to time I can use it to send a message for you."

07:31 PM

Thank you. I am watching the news.

07:52 PM

186 *********

This is the tracking number for the funds. I sent ***$

Wed, May 15 08:52 AM

I hope it helps. Thinking of you.

12:34 PM

Let me know when you receive it

01:04 PM

Audio: "I will be in contact to tell you everything. Thank you, thank you so much."

I hope we will raise more.

Thu, May 16 06:44 AM

Good evening how are you

I want to tell you that today I will receive the money after two hours

I'm glad. Thank you for telling me.

Thanks so much for you and everyone

We are trying to help in the little ways we can.

Even if it is a little, it means a lot to us, you know that

Yes. We hope this

Thank you.

Thanks God that you're here

I hope God will help me do more.

Ameen

Fri, May 17 05:10 AM

Video of Amira flashing a peace sign.

05:28 AM

Video with audio: Amira sitting along a wall with friends and family members. "Serene, the little child Eiman, my brother Mohammad, and there is Allene."

Photos 31I, 31J, and 31K.

Photo 31L: an orange-and-white mama cat licking the face of her kitten as they sit on Amira's lap.

07:03 AM

Two kitties!!

10:00 AM

I found it

I love that

Mon, May 20 09:44 PM

Hi Amira

I am checking in on you.

10:55 PM

Hi dear how are you

We are OK Al Hamdallah

Ok. Thank you.

Tue, May 21 01:01 AM

Wed, May 22 08:31 AM

How are you

12:51 PM

Good evening how are you

We are fine still in Rafah

01:19 PM

Ok Thank God. I will be checking every day.

Thu, May 23, 02:18 AM

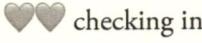

07:31 AM

checking in

07:59 AM

Good evening I'm in Deir al-Balah with my grandfather

08:54 AM

What happened?

Nothing, he had come to visit us and spent two days with us, and I decided to return with him to Deir al-Balah and spend two days with my uncles.

Ok. This is good, yes?

In order to go to visit my aunt and her two daughters who were martyred, she is buried in the Deir al-Balah cemetery, and my birthday and hers fall on the same day, 5/30, but she is ten years older than me.

Photo 31A

Photo 31B

Photo 31C

Photo 31D

Photo 31E

Photo 31F

Photo 31H

Photo 31G

Photo 31I

Photo 31J

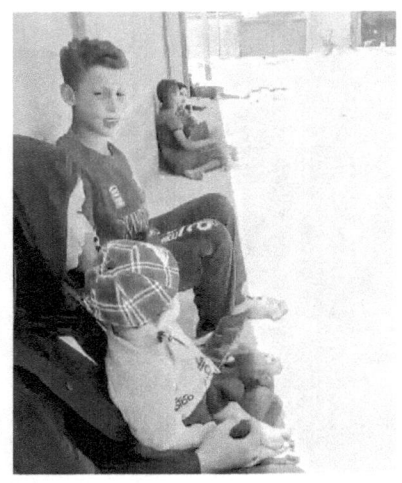

Photo 31K

Photo 31L

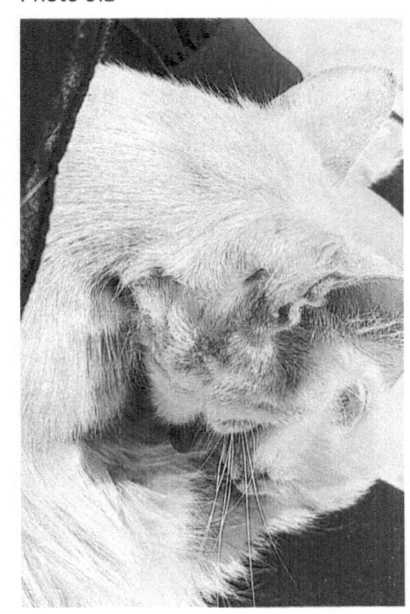

CHAPTER 32
RESISTANCE AND SPIRIT IN THE CLASSROOM

We remain what is left in us, a breath of life
Everything dies in us and we are still standing
It is power but there's no other choice
No time to grieve, no time to be weak, not even to collapse
Here we are in Gaza like the phoenix living from the ashes

Sun, May 26 06:09 AM

Audio: "Hello dear, how are you and I wish you are okay and in good health. I'm sorry I was not in contact with you in the last day. The internet and the connection here is not very good. I was writing about here and the place and the school where my grandmother is. I will send it for you when I translate, and some pictures from the place, and some pictures for the children here. They are studying in the same class where they use it for sleep, and they use it for learn. I was writing about that, about the place, about Deir al-Balah, about new life. It is a different life about that than we have in Rafah or in the tent. Many people, they are still in the tent, but in different way, and difficult way. It is not very good, but I will send it for you, and after that we will talk. I wish you are okay, and for remember this day I am still thinking: How will my new year will be. You know after a few days I will become twenty–seven years old. I hope it will come with different things, with good things. I hope. I don't know, but I hope."

08:16 AM

Audio: "Thank you thank you thank you. I am very excited to see those pictures. I can't wait to see them. Thank you so much for thinking of me and sending them. Yeah, I think I saw something on Instagram about the children learning in the school in Deir al-Balah. I'm sorry, my pronunciation is terrible, but I think it's Deir Al- Balah. I thought that's what you said. I saw that they were holding classes there and I thought . . . This is Palestinian Resistance! I know we hear this term a lot, Palestinian Resistance. I hope that people can understand what that really truly means. Because in the midst of all of the chaos and the war, still people are holding classes for the children. Incredible. Thank you."

12:30 PM

Four photos from Amira—32A, 32B, 32C, and 32D—show the students learning in the classroom.

Sunday, May 26, 2024

"War and Hope"

We still have life, and we continue to fight and love life as much as we can here in the ranks of this school inhabited by displaced people. The journey of education resumed after long periods of interruption. Some teachers decided to establish classes for children in kindergarten and first grade, providing them with the basics and following up with them in the same place where people stay overnight. In the morning, children attend the school with enthusiasm, love, and passion, unlike those filled with rules, regulations, and adherence to a specific dress code and schedule for each teaching session. They have the freedom to choose the clothes they wear, colorful and beautiful, with smiling faces. They sit on the ground with only a notebook and a pen, resembling a university in a way, but on a smaller scale, open to generations unaware of their future and their day. Many of them have lost their most precious belongings, but they love what they do: participating, singing, and playing. I thought of giving them simple gifts to encourage them, so I brought some sweets to distribute to them, and how happy I was about it, as if they had won a big prize.

Photo 32E: a view across the top of the tent city at dusk. The sky's colors look like pastels from a Monet painting.

"A New Experience... A Greater Tragedy"

I had decided to go to the city of Deir al-Balah to spend some time with my grandfather and his family, my uncles, aunts, and their children, and to meet some friends and relatives who were present in Deir al-Balah, having fled the war. I returned with my grandfather, who was visiting us for two days. He and his family stayed in a UNRWA school that had become a center for sheltering displaced people from all areas of the Gaza Strip. It was filled with a large number of families. It had a specific system like other schools, where classrooms were a place for women and children to sleep and live, and downstairs in the schoolyard, there were many tents for sleeping and staying for men and youth.

Life here is terrible, full of tragedy and gradual death. Eight months in a place where basic necessities like water, electricity, and others are scarcely available. You have to wait in long lines at certain hours to get drinkable water and water for cleaning, among other things. The walls have lost their colors and acquired blackness due to the frequent use of stoves for cooking and boiling water. Worse yet is the use of bathrooms that are never clean, and even if they are cleaned, they quickly become dirty due to the frequent use and overcrowding, and the lack of water and cleaning supplies, with no maintenance available.

We toured the city of Deir al-Balah, this small city that was always beautiful, full of trees and green spaces, and its inhabitants were farmers living their lives peacefully. Now, every place in it is crowded and filled with tents and noise;

there's no empty space, not even the beach, which is not spared from the displaced. It's a huge population explosion, and this war seems endless. There are no landmarks for it.

In Gaza, death is one, even if its forms and causes are numerous. And as each day passes in this month, I wonder how a new year added to my life will be, and in what condition will it come? How will I welcome my 27th year in a few days? 💔🥹

Saturday, 26/5/2024

Amira Alzaneen

Tue, May 28, 06:37 AM

Amira, is today your birthday? Or is it in 2 more days?

I didn't realize I had not answered your above messages. I sent them to friends, but I did not answer you!

This is a powerful image of the children and the teacher in the school. I love it. I love that you brought them sweets. That was a wonderful thing to do.

05:49 PM

Audio: "Good evening dear, how are you? After two days is my birthday. I will become twenty-seven years old in the last of May. I hope it will be good things will happen in that day. I don't know, I come here to Rafah yesterday because the situation was very bad with my family, and I come to see them and to stay with them. Last night was very bad in Rafah. The bombing and explosion was near us here in the tent. Many people die. Everywhere is dangerous. We are looking for a safe place to go for it. We will travel maybe to Asda. It is in Khan Younis. We will look for a place in there to sit in it. I am so happy and so proud that it is a beautiful thing that the children are learning in this situation, in this war. They still have a hope to continue their life. I'm very happy about that. I will answer you after I have a good internet. It is so bad, the connection. I will tell you everything when we return for another place or stay here." [During this conversation, the Israeli drones/planes are constant and loud overhead.]

Thank you Amira. I am hearing the brightness of your soul coming through again.

Photo 32A

Photo 32B

Photo 32C

Photo 32E

Photo 32D

CHAPTER 33
HAPPY BIRTHDAY, BOOK TITLES, AND ANOTHER DISPLACEMENT

Pat your heart with your hand, the world's hand is busy.

Thu, May 30 06:17 AM

Audio: "Happiest of birthdays to you, Amira. I know you are in a difficult position, but it is your birthday. Happy twenty-seventh. And I want you to know that although you are faced with extreme difficulties, the contributions that you are already making are incredible and inspiring, and I'm very, very proud to know you. Happy Birthday."

07:37 AM

Hi how are you

Up and preparing for work.

Thinking about your birthday.

Thank you so much

10:22 AM

Audio: "Thank you, thank you for everything. I'm proud to have friends like you. I'm proud, I'm so proud to have you in my life. I'm so happy to be beginning a new year in my life, and have friends. Have someone care for me. I wish the new year will be different, will be good, will be happy."

Audio: "I feel the same way. I'm very proud to have you as my friend, and I share your work with others. We are still working on this book. Have faith, we are working on the book. We have two titles now; I want you to think about it. The first one is So Remember Me: Witness Gaza. *The second one is, my son Roland thought of it,* I Am No Longer Afraid to Die: Witness Gaza. *I wonder if you have a choice."*

Photos 33A and 33B: a now-abandoned Ferris wheel in the town across the dirt lot that now houses the tent city of refugees. Amira, her mother, and a sister smiling as they sit outside their tent.

Audio: "I think he said I Am Not Afraid to Die *or* I Am No Longer Afraid to Die *because I think that you wrote to me—you did write in one of your messages that you were no longer afraid to die because you knew you would go on in this book, and my son said, "That's a great book title!* I Am No Longer Afraid to Die. *So just think about it,* I Am No Longer Afraid to Die *or* So Remember Me. *I like them both. Maybe it will come to you which one you would like."*

Audio: "That's so difficult. I don't know, the two titles are so beautiful, so different, the same message. I Am Not Afraid to Die, So Remember Me, they are connected to others. The idea I'm not afraid to die, so remember me, I don't know. I will let you choose, you can see from my writing what's better. I will write something new about the travelling from Rafah to Khan Younis and send it for you when I have time to write. You know that . . . after that we try to [sigh and short laugh] stay in this place and know it. After that I will write the story. [Deep sigh.] It was so hard."

Audio: *"I'm laughing because the people near us are looking and laugh for me because I speak English. This is something different, something—[laughing]—I don't know how to describe this but they are looking for me and asking what I say.*

"Yes, I guess the title that your son choose, it's very beautiful and very different and have a big message. And the other title, So Remember Me, a little title—maybe 'So Remember Me,' we can take it as a message to end the book. In the end of the book, we can say a message for everyone that I tell you before, the many messages for the end we can use 'So Remember Me.' And use the title that your son choose, because it's very beautiful."

12:23 PM

My friends are sending you Happy Birthday wishes!

Happy birthday to Amira! [Forwarded from friends]

Happy birthday to Amira!! [Forwarded from friends]

12:40 PM

Audio: *"Oh, thank you, thank you very much. Happy life for you."*

Sun, June 2 07:05 AM

Good morning Amira. How are you today?

10:42 AM

Hi dear I'm fine what about you??

I'm ok. Checking on you!

Audio: *"Maybe a little better than the few days that go. The* new place, it's good. I don't know, we hope we can come back for our home, but to safety. Travelling from place to place. Scared from bombing, dangers. I don't know, but everything is well. We try to know the new place well."

11:13 AM

Audio: "I have a friend. She was asking me many times, 'Are you okay for real?' For a moment, I just stop and thinking . . . How. Are. Me. At this time. To be honest, I'm not okay, I'm not fine, not better. Everything is not good. Everything is very bad, everything is very hard. It's so difficult, escaping from place to place, thinking if the next day will come, how it will be? If we will survive or die? We don't know. Lose some friends, lose some love. We lose everything and still afraid from losing more. It's tiring. How getting our food, our water, traveling for another place, it's safety, it's dangerous; many things thinking of it. It's hard. And fill me with pain. I miss my life. I miss my brother. I miss my friends, I miss my work, I miss many things. Trying to be strong, trying to be okay. Need for a big power to do that. Smiling or crying, it is an emotion that I don't know how to do it. Many people try to continue their day. And that's what we do. Just thinking, how will this day go on. That we will we survive or not. That we will have a new day or not. I don't know. The answer is very hard, very difficult. It's like you are running and running and running and you don't have time to take a breath or not. Your heart bump very hard. You don't know if you have time to take a breath or not. You don't know if the bad thing is after you. You just continue. Running and running. Don't look for your left, your right. You don't know anything. Just want to be safety. Just want to continue your day without knowing anything. It's like, I don't know, it's very impossible. I don't know how we can live that."

12:50 PM

I often think about how it must be to live with almost total loss and uncertainty. As you said, to miss everything, and to never know if the bad thing is after you. To never know what will happen as you sleep. To witness your own suffering and those around you without having enough resources to help.

I am sorry for the evil that has been let loose in Gaza. I hope too that it will end. Soon. 💔 🖤 🤍

I hope that so much

Audio: "Yes. Many times I think that if we survive from this war, we need a whole time to wake up from this nightmare, and to come back to our life. To be a normal human. We need many things to come for our life. I don't know if we can. But if we will survive, we will try. It's not easy. Really, it's not easy."

Thu, June 6 01:31 AM

How are you

Hi Amira. I am awake for some reason. Maybe to talk to you.

Audio: "Good morning. How are you, I wish you are ok and everything is well. I don't know. I just wanted to talk to you. The situation here is not very well. As a start, like a beginning, is a thing new. Here the place is good but still we look for water as we start in Rafah. Nothing new in the news."

Oh good morning

For two day I don't use the internet

It is 1:35 in the morning here. I just woke up for no reason.

I have been thinking about you and how to respond. What words to comfort you? How to encourage you? Every message now, I feel your pain. I hear your exhaustion.

I will always be here, listening to you. Praying for you. Wishing I could be there to hug you

Pain and fatigue have become a common thing for most. It is hidden in my heart and it hurts me so much and I cannot stay. It is not possible to stop now. There is still time that we must continue. Everything is not over. I do not know when, but there must be an end to it. I trust that.

People are still fighting for you every day. Many brave young people still. No matter what, your beautiful soul will be remembered.

Human beings are blinded by greed and fear. They believe the lies of the media. Please know that more and more are seeing truth. I pray you survive every day. I also know your faith goes beyond this crazy world.

I am certain that God does not give us more than we can bear, and that in the Holy Qur'an, God does not burden a soul with more than it can bear, meaning that we are able to endure and succeed in tests of patience, and everything will become better, and God will not abandon us.

I love you. You are a light in this world.

Me to. I love you so much and proud to have someone like you in my life 🤍

I am here for you.

02:15 AM

When coming here from Rafah in the city of Asda, in fact, it is a city of games and entertainment previously. It was as if we were displaced the first time. We started again. We moved with everything we had brought since our stay in Rafah. We went back to wait to fill water and search for wood for the fire, the market, etc. The move was expensive. The truck needed approximately $400 and repairing the tents, the place, etc. everything was exhausted. This is the most difficult. But we are still trying to adapt. I don't know how, but we are trying

The truck driver charged 400 Dollars???

This is small compared to other cheap trucks, others ask for more than 2000 shekels and a lot. Since fuel is very expensive and there is no gas, this is normal. Because of the danger, everyone was forced to leave and look for another place.

Photo 33C: loading up a truck with the encampment of Amira's family.

It is hot. Not a single tree so I see.

This was in Rafah, a desert area. Two days after we moved, it was destroyed and the army arrived there. There is no green area there.

02:44 AM

How did you know you had to leave?

03:01 AM

When the army's military operation began in Rafah, the displaced began to dismantle their tents and leave and search for another, safer place. We did not leave at first, but we stayed, and the place began to empty and become empty of people day after day, until a crazy night happened again, and the bombardment and gunfire everywhere, and the army got very close. There was a bombing in the place near the displaced people, and many were killed, and the artillery was bombing randomly. When the morning came, everyone decided to leave and leave after the children and adults were frightened, and no one remained. The place had no soul without the people. It became scary. There was no water, no hospital, and nothing. We decided to go somewhere else, even though the conditions were bad, but no. Escape

07:02 AM

My friend Michael in Italy has been translating your work to Italian and sharing.

I want you to know that we feel you as much as we can.

08:24 AM

09:10 AM

Photo 33D: people standing around a water hose with their water containers, an inoperable Ferris wheel in the background. This is the town of Asda, Gaza, in Khan Younis. It used to be an amusement park.

Audio: "Today, the water is free here in this place. Today they have come with water for people who came for Asda City and sit after travelling from Rafah, from Khan Younis, from many places, and came here to be safe. Some get some water for a little money and after that and many hours can the people come and take water as you see in the post. It is near the tent, not far. It's good because nobody have water in his tent. Need for water for food, for cleaning, for many things, you know that. I don't know, we were using the internet and the water you see, behind us."

09:27 AM

I'm happy there is water!

How are you getting food?

Audio: "For that, it's not easy. Sometimes we go to Deir al-Balah for marketing the food that we need because the center for many things that we buy is in Deir al-Balah. Here in the place, because you know Khan Younis was attacked before from Israelian, nothing is good. Everything is destroyed. No marketing, no place. [It] is an empty place. For that, if we have money, we need something, we go for Deir al-Balah and buy everything we need. A little. Not many things, but a little. The water works for maybe one hour a day for people can get it for free. They still work to have everyone here to get it. It's a very good thing. Many times we cannot find clean water to drink. Now the weather is very hot. You know we need to take a shower many times. I don't know, but I hope the next day the situation will be better and better than that. It's the first time in this place, and you know the first time every time it is difficult."

Have you heard from Osama?

Audio: "I speak with him today and yesterday. The situation in the north is so bad, very very bad. No food, no water. Nothing is good. They are traveling from place to place, the bombing, the exploding everywhere. He don't have any money, for sorry. He ask, but for sorry, we don't have. He go from north to Gaza [City] looking for some food, for some clean water, some safety, we don't know. They stay sometimes in the north, sometimes in Gaza, sometimes in another place. I hope. Hope we can see him very soon, and he will be okay, and God take care of him."

I am glad Hassan is with you. I pray he sees his father again.

Audio: "Hassan is with us. He ask about him and he just asking us to care for them, and be careful with him. He miss him so much. He loves to see him, he ask for many pictures. I don't know, I hope he will come soon and see him and hug him every day that we are in another place, together."

Thinking of you.

I'm OK

Audio: "I'm fine, or, trying to be. The weather here is very hot. The situation is not very good. Nothing new. We lose some of our cousins in the north. We cannot contact with Osama. We don't know, we don't know when this war will end, when everything will stop, when our lose become the last one. Time to time we lose many things."

Audio: [She is crying.] "Hi, dear. How are you? I wish you are okay. Today I am in a bad situation. I... I... we just was talking to Osama in the north. Today we lose two brothers from our cousin. We cannot talk with Osama, for many days we do not know anything. We just know they are killed this morning, in home, bombing, and they are, was, in it. Motaz and Amerad, brothers, were in it and they die. For sorry. Before minutes, we was talk to Osama. He's okay, but not very okay. He was crying. He was with Motaz and Amerad for twenty days. He left them yesterday and go to another place. They stay in the place, and the Israelian killed them. He was crying and say for me, 'You should take care for my wife and my son Hassan. My mother, my sister, my brother. We don't know what will happen the next day. I don't know if I can see them, or see anyone, or come back for the home.' I just feel pain, and cry, like my heart go out from its place. I'm scared. I'm very scared. I miss Osama. I want him to be safe and be okay. I want to see him after this war will end. He speak with my mom, with my sister, and want them to forgive him, and to pray for him, and to take care with his son. I don't know, but he is tired. He is very very tired. He is scaring. [Deep sigh, crying still.] I know that night I was with Osama at the home. It was very very bad. I feel that I shouldn't [have] left him for the north and come for the south. I ask myself why I don't stay with him there. Why I leave? He need for us. He is afraid that is the war is for the whole time. He is tired, and ask if we will survive all the time or not. I hope, hope and pray for God, help him, and save him, and protect him until we come back and see him and hug him. This is something so bad. We want this war will stop. We, I don't know, but we are scared from losing more from people that we love. Or have another shock to lose someone for us. I wish, I don't know when this war will end, but I hope that will happen very very soon."

04:11 AM

I am sending you all the love I have. I don't know how much a person can endure.

Your voice will be heard. Osama will be known. You will have a legacy.

Audio: "I'm sure we will be a story, that all the world will remember it and talk about it. We are not just a number. We are a human. All of us have a story. All the world should know it. We have all reason to love and live in this life. We are, as all the humans in this world, have many things to do. Have many dreams, have many. We just want to survive. We just want to live, we just want to come back for our life. To be a normal people. I don't know how, but I hope. I hope this will end very soon. Stop losing, stop scaring, stop moving from place to place. The dangers go away. Our heart not afraid. I hope. But sometimes I feel I just want screaming . . . crying . . . run away . . . looking for another place to cry, to meet. I don't know. There's no time for that. No time. When he talk to me yesterday, I just fall down. I don't have any power. It was very hard. I hope he will be okay, he will be safety, I will see him very soon."

Mon, June 10 03:33 AM

Audio: "Hello dear, how are you? I wish you are okay. I know the time now is very different between us. Maybe it is night, maybe you are sleeping. I just remember I was telling you I want to write about travelling from Rafah to Khan Younis, this place. But because I was busy with Osama, with what's happening in the north, with staying here in the new place, I wasn't wrote anything. For sorry. But when I do that, I will send it very soon. I hope everything will be okay and everything will end very soon, and we will be strong until this moment. After that we can be weak, we can cry, we can do many things. [Deep sigh.] We can take our breath."

07:02 AM

When you can. We are listening every day to your words. I send them to people here and my friend in Italy. He shares with his network. Even before the book, people are reading and listening.

We all love you and think about you. Thank you for sharing even the little things. We are listening to you.

Tue, June 11 09:06 AM

Audio: "Hi there. Thank you, thank you so much. That make me proud, very happy to know that someone in this world know our stories, listen for us, know that we are still here, we are alive, we are surviving. We are trying to be safety, we are trying to be good feelings. I'm sure the day will come, I will meet all the people who know Amira, who know what we are living in Gaza. Who want to listen to us, and see us face to face. To thank them for all supporting, for thinking of us. For all love for that. I hope that day will come very soon."

11:05 AM

Hello my dear. How is your day?

02:09 PM

Audio: "Good evening, dear, and how is your day? [Deep sigh.] To be honest, I don't know. But it is just day and eve, end like the other days. Tired, but Humdalalah for everything. Thanks for God, and hope the next day will be good, will be different."

02:40 PM

Yes. Every day. We hope for the next better day. At least we still have hope.

Wed, June 12 02:21 AM

Audio: "Yes, exactly. That's what we say every time. That thanks for God that we still have a hope. We are still smiling, try to be okay, try to be strong, everything will be better. We still waiting for the news about if they accept the new things for in the war. We hope that it will end very soon."

03:55 AM

Hello, how are you. I think a lot. The blessed Eid Al-Adha is approaching. I do not know how we will spend it in these tiring circumstances

Sat, June 15 09:56 AM

Hi Amira. My thoughts are with you today. I am wishing you to have a spark of joy somewhere in this day.

12:21 PM

Hi dear I will try do that at night

12:51 PM

Audio: "Good evening, Jeannie, and how is your day? I wish you are ok. It is a good idea. Tomorrow is Eid Adah Mubarak. I guess I can go at night, do that. Go away. Maybe."

02:05 PM

Audio "Hi, Amira. I'm not sure what you mean that you can go at night for something? Also, we collected a little more money, so let me know how to get it to you."

Audio: "Hello, dear, good evening. How are you? I mean that tomorrow is Eid for Muslim. I don't know what they say in English. It is the big Eid, and we go out this night and walk, as a journey, to get energy and power, a good power, see our friends, see our family. Try to be happy, try to be safety. A little thing makes a big difference, you know. About sending money, that's can."

I'll tell you when I receive the donation so I can send you. Today people donated more to our fund. It is for you.

Audio: "Thank you so much. Thank you for all the people who did it, who support, who are thinking of us. A little thing, it's

so different, and big different. All love for you, and I hope the new day will come with happy things."

Mon, June 17 07:04 AM

Hi Amira. How is it going today?

08:25 AM

Hi dear I'm ok what about you

10:03 AM

Ok. Waiting on a few more funds to arrive.

Wed, June 19 02:48 PM

Hi how are you

Hi hi hi!!! Thinking about you. How are you?

04:01 PM

Are you there?

Thu, June 20 02:36 AM

The internet so bad

04:29 AM

Audio: "We just hear explosions and bombing everywhere. We don't know where, but we see in the news it is in Rafah, the place that we were in there. Hope everything will be okay, will be better. The connection is so bad, because of that, I cannot use the internet every time. Just a little time, maybe at night it will be okay. I'm sorry that, but I just want to be without [laughs, inaudible].

[230] AMIRA ALZANEEN AND JEANNIE AMASH

[Fifteen seconds later.] Hi, good evening, how are you? I'm okay, fine, trying to be better. The situation in Rafah so bad, we don't know what will happening, we just hear—" [Cut off.]

Photo 33A

Photo 33B

Photo 33C

Photo 33D

CHAPTER 34
A LITTLE LAUGHTER

*Do not make my company a misery, my presence a burden,
or my speech harmful. My Lord, make me easy to follow,
my influence lasting, and provide me with beautiful sustenance,
content, happy, and prosperous wherever I may be, O God.*

Sat, June 22 05:45 AM

*Audio: "Hi, Amira. I'm sorry, I didn't realize that I didn't respond
to your last message. I've been thinking about you every day. I'm glad
you were able to leave Rafah. Yes, I've seen on the news that you,
not you, but that Rafah is being targeted by Israel, even though they
said it was a safe zone. Israel is continuing to break their word. I'm
very sorry that you have to listen to this bombing, and that you are
in such chaos and uncertainty in your life. I am thinking about you
every single day, and again I apologize that I didn't respond. I just
woke up and checked my messages to see if you messaged me and I
realized that I had not answered you. So message when you can. I
look forward to hearing from you every single day."*

01:09 PM

Audio: "Hi dear, good evening. How are you? I wish that you
are okay. I'm sorry I could not connect with you the last day,
the internet was so bad. We are okay, trying to be safety as

we can. The Israelian still attack Rafah. The situation there so bad, the explosion, bombing, they destroy everything. But we are here in Khan Younis, Asda City. Just listening for bombing away from us. We hope everything will end very soon. We hope everything come back to the normal life. Trying to survive as we can. Thank you for your ask. Thank you for thinking of me. I'm happy to listen to your voice. I will contact you if I can when the internet will be better than that. Thank you so much. Today we do something in the sea, for the children, here in Khan Younis. I will send for you some photos to see it. It was very beautiful, very laughing."

Multiple photos (34A, 34B, 34C, 34D, 34E, 34F, 34G) of people dressed in bright clown costumes, some with painted faces and wigs. They dance, clap, and perform for the crowd of children and adults gathered to watch. Photos of some of the children, their skin deeply bronzed from the sun, that were watching the performances. Surely these are the performers who used to work at the carnivals and amusement park in Asda, which is now a refugee tent city.

Sun, June 23 06:52 AM

Audio: "To be honest with you, at this day we cannot understand exactly the news, what happening in any place in this area. We just trying to be safe from danger. No place is safe 100 percent. Every place had some bombing any time. The Israelian, you know about that, Rafah situation is so bad. North, others, they are hungry, they are so hungry. Nothing food, or aid go there. Here, everything is expensive. We have, but so expensive. Thinking how, or what will happen for the future. Ehh . . . we just have a little hope everything will end. We just trying to still be strong. We are."

Mon, June 24 01:57 PM

Did this make you smile?

Audio: "Absolutely. This is seeing children happy, and do something for them in this situation. Exactly. It makes me *very happy. It makes me to forget what we live now. It was such a beautiful day. All of them, children, women, and guys, they are on the beach, was so happy. I love doing that. It was doing that, not so expensive. They just take $200 to do that for two and a half hours. And this thing makes many people so happy, so kind, and—I don't know how to say that, but using playing, laughing, song. They get out from the strange, and the situation that's bad in this war."*

Fri, June 28 07:40 AM

Amira Amira where are you?

I'm here how are you

Can I still send money for you?

Thank God you are there!

I'm OK

Can I send it to you?

08:04 AM

Audio: "Send it at my name in Gaza. Authority of Palestine. You know that. All information with you, isn't it?"

I can do that. Good good.

I would love to talk soon. Now I am preparing for work. We will talk soon

Yes, I have all the information.

Audio: "Okay, I will wait for that time when we talk. Be careful and okay. Um, I'm fine. We have a visitor. My uncle and children. Many people here. I will talk to you and tell you what is happening if you want to know anything. Thank God, I'm okay. And Osama is very good. Thank you."

Can we talk in about 2 hours? I will have time at work

Absolutely I will try to have good internet

Great!!

Are you there?

Yes

:([after two failed attempts at calling Amira] I'm sorry! I will try again

Finally, Amira and I connected via video call, although we were cut off within a minute. We tried and succeeded two more times for a minute each. She showed me around the outside and inside of the large tent housing her family. One corner had been sectioned off for her mother and father, and each family unit/member had followed suit. The bedding was on the ground, blankets and clothing neatly folded on top. I was struck at how orderly it all was. In spite of the chaos, they kept their tents neat and as clean as possible. This is traditional Palestinian style. Homes are customarily kept very clean with daily scrubbing and mopping of the floors, sinks, and bathrooms. Tiles are kept gleaming. Carpets vacuumed. Here, even though there is obviously no access to such cleaning, everything was still neat, folded, and organized.

You've become Bedouins

Audio: "I hate that. I hate when the internet connection is so bad. I cannot speak with you better. It just cut and cut and cut. This is the place, the new tent that we are arrive from Rafah to here. We try to design it as a small room, for my father, my mother, the girl, my brother Fadi and his wife. Oh, trying to feel that we are in home. Be free."

Audio: [laughing] "Yes, yes! From the hot, our skin is black. Day after day, I don't know, it's not normal. Like the Bedouins' tent. Another thing, looking for many things as Bedouins."

Sun, June 30 08:28 AM

Are you OK???

Yes yes! I'm sorry, the money didn't send. I will do it again today. I am working a lot and got distracted.

You will have it soon.

08:54 AM

It's OK no problem

10:09 AM

382*******

Sent! Here is your number

11:21 AM

***$

12:43 PM

Thank you so much

01:13 PM

You are welcome

Mon, July 1 10:12 AM

Audio: "Hi, Amira! This is Jeannie, your friend in America! [Laughs.]

Hey, just checking to make sure you received the money, or that you are able to get it. Let me know if you are able to get it. Thank you."

05:30 PM

Good evening how are you absolutely I will get it tomorrow

Great!

Wed, July 3 09:03 AM

Did you get it?

Fri, July 5 03:30 AM

Are you there?

03:47 AM

Good morning how are you

Yes I have it

I know. I got the notification.

I want to know how are you, how is everyone? Did you say Osama was doing ok?

I know the internet is terrible.

Photo 34A

Photo 34B

Photo 34C

Photo 34D

Photo 34E

Photo 34F

Photo 34G

CHAPTER 35
OSAMA HELPS PROVIDE WATER IN THE NORTH

We can only be truly successful at things we are willing to fail at,
and if we are not willing to fail, we are not willing to succeed at all.

06:53 AM

Audio: "Good evening. How are you and how is your day? Everyone here is good, we are fine. I was sick. I was have a flu very bad. I get in the bed for two days. Osama is okay. The situation better in the last day in the north. Exactly, the internet connection is so bad. I'm okay, and I miss you so much, and I want to thank you for everything."

07:25 AM

Osama sent part of the amount, approximately 800 shekels, to carry out the distribution of potable water in a center to shelter the displaced in the north.

08:04 AM

Wish I was with you. Be well soon. Rest.

Audio: "You are with me all the time, and every day, and ev-

ery situation you are with me. The rest will come at the best time. I'm sure about that. We will have to take a rest, to have our breath, to be okay, to come back strong. [Deep sigh.] We will do everything. But in the perfect time."

Sun, July 7 06:19 AM

How are you

06:41 AM

Ok how are you today Amira?

I'm OK

I'm glad.

You say Osama is ok?

Yes he is fine

I'm glad Amira.

The work that he did it in the North.

Photos 35A, 35B, 35C: Many people are standing behind a water tank truck. They are in a line with their yellow five-gallon (or twenty-liter) water jugs.

07:38 AM

Can you explain to me how people organized these trucks?

In the north, you know there are famines and a lack of availability of water, food, and other basic necessities, but fortunately there were still some working water wells and intact trucks that were not affected. Their owners worked to distribute water to shelter centers, relying on external donations, as they needed a source of energy, fuel, etc. to transport and withdraw water. From the well

I sent the amount to Osama in the north, approximately

$200, which went to the owners of the cart and the well and paid them to go to a shelter center where people were and fill water for them for free.

Some trucks run on cooking oil instead of unavailable fuel

08:38 AM

Were some of the funds we sent you used for this?? This makes me so happy!!!

Me to, so so happy

I am so proud. So proud of you that you are sharing this money, to help others. I am proud of you to tears. You are a Superhero.

Thanks so much for everything 🩶

I am crying. I am so proud to know you.

I'm who so proud to have you in my life

Photo 35A

Photo 35B

Photo 35C

CHAPTER 36
THE UNBEARABLE HAPPENS

I don't want to end up in a bag!!
I give up everything... except my death
I want a full shroud, 192 cm long.
I will not give up my paradise, I want it complete
I want my arms, my feet, my heart, my head,
my twenty fingers, and my eyes too...
I want to return to the womb of the earth,
as I was created from it.. the same earth here in this
Country.. I don't mind being buried in a mass grave.
But I want my name on the witness, my age as well,
and that I am from here, from this slaughtered homeland...
I would like, with all my bitterness, for my grave to be in a real
cemetery, not a street, not a sidewalk, not anything else...
As our last wish and right... farewell
In it
All we wish and want.

Wed, July 10

Grief

There is no solace for those who mourn their losses. Even

tears can hardly suffice for the enormity of the anguish and pain that crushes the heart. We almost forget how to unleash our grief and sorrows.

We've been trapped inside for so long, releasing in sighs that uproot what remains of the soul, slowly dying more each day. The days continue to pass; the war has not stopped.

As if death is commonplace, every day the sun rises on a new day. They are not just numbers; each victim has a story, each death a method and an extinguishing.

Brief farewell moments in hospital corridors, on roads, or beneath rubble. Things haven't changed for more than two hundred and seventy-five days.

And the sword reaches out, snatching lives in all its forms from everywhere. These days, it's a vile and sickening epidemic without a cure, sadness without joy, loss without reunion.

Farewells marred by parting, and days continue to march into the unknown, bereaved in some stories, missing in others. This ghost city can no longer contain such a torrent of pain.

The river of blood hasn't ceased for a moment. We are the witnesses and the witnessed, the event itself in all its corners, the narrators and those narrated about. We've all tasted the bitterness of this war without exception.

Truly, those who survived have lost, and those who died have survived in this city. 💔

 Amira Alzaneen

Wed, July 10 06:38 AM

Osama

Osama was exposed to an explosion in the north. He is in the hospital and dying

09:48 AM

I lose my brother 💔

I cannot imagine. He is your hero, I know. He is the one who stands for you, the one you love.

I am with you today day. I am beyond sorry. I carry your heartbreak. My brave friend Amira.

10:56 AM

Photo 36A: Osama's body is wrapped in a bloody white sheet, his lifeless face exposed. A man touches his face as others look on.

Oh God I'm sorry.

11:14 AM

I am crying with you.

Thu, July 11 02:24 AM

Audio: [crying] "I don't know what to say, I don't know how to say that, but my loss is so big. I feel that I lost my life, I'm dying, that my heart is not working, that it came out from the place. I cannot believe that. That Osama, he go. I know that he is in a better place. He's fine now. He is not tired, but I miss him, I need him. I still need him in my life. He wanted to die like that, and he get it. I cannot say goodbye. I want to see him another time. Maybe in the heaven. I don't know. But he deserves heaven."

08:34 AM

Crying with you. He deserves heaven.

08:57 AM

09:07 AM

I'm sorry. I feel your loss. I feel you from across the sea.

09:53 AM

11:12 AM

Amira, if you can, write about this.

11:30 AM

Photo 36B: Headshot of Osama from when Jeannie visited Amira and Osama and family in Gaza, 2022.

He is with you.

11:47 AM

Audio: "To be honest with you, I don't know if I can write about this. I cannot imagine that I'm lose Osama. I wasn't think about that anytime. But if I write about this, the title will be, 'He Deserve, He Really Deserve the Heaven.' He really was doing everything beautiful for the people in the north. He was give them the food, the water. He was going from place to place to get some food for the people in the school. He do what he can for everyone. He was a beautiful man. He was protect me every time. He stood behind me in my sadness and my happiness. He stood for everything. I don't know, I don't know what will be talking about this. I didn't mention that I will listen for this news, that one day I will lose Osama. I cannot say goodbye for him. I cannot hug him. I cannot take him in my hand, but you know. He's a good man, deserve everything beautiful."

Photo 36A

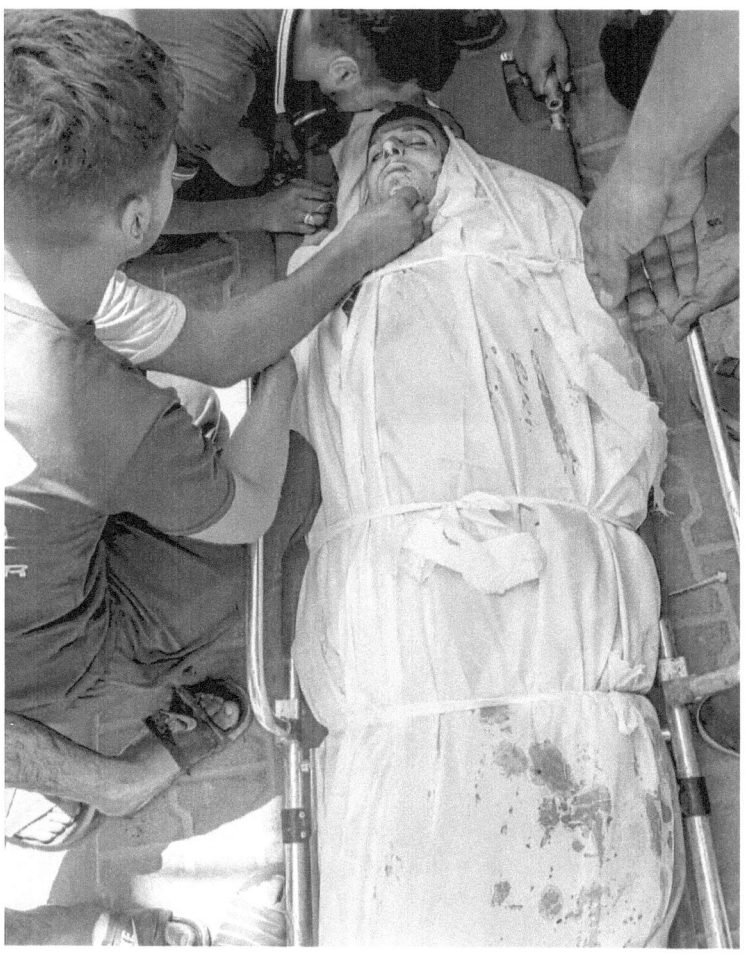

Photo 36B

CHAPTER 37
HE DESERVES PARADISE

My tears reached its barrier
I miss you, and the loss of death is bitter and fragrant
My consolation and my heart's patience
is that you are in a paradise you deserve
My soul is healed by a meeting and an embrace in my dreams
Making me repeat: "Oh, if only we could repeat it in the afterlife"
Sometimes life makes you think you're a rock,
but you're really a branch that even a gentle breeze can blow away.

I never imagined my loss would be this immense, ripping my heart out of its place. It's my soul that has lost. We survived a lot together, fought wars side by side. We never parted. I remember that night at home, he was by my side, looking at me. That look won't leave me; he was afraid for me, trying to protect me, feeling helpless. Those times he went searching for food and water to feed people in shelters and children, risking himself, never sleeping, never thinking of himself. I met him in moments, he'd contact me if he needed something. Even when we moved places in Gaza before going south, he'd walk miles to see me, to get some rest and food I'd scour the streets to give to him when he came. It made him so happy to get dates or a small box of beans. We stayed like this until we decided to leave for the south, and his wife and child were supposed to join us but refused to leave him. I sent food and supplies to an empty house so he could pick them up from there. I wanted to flee and return to him, but it didn't happen, and during the 276-day war he never left me for a day. I tried my best to provide for him from afar, my heart afraid each time he went out or disappeared, praying to God to protect and save him. Even during the famine in the north, when there was no food or drink, and Ramadan began, his wife and child returned, and I brought them to stay with my family, but he couldn't join us and stayed in the north. Many details connect me to my first love, my support, and my hero, and everything beautiful in my life. I used to wake up to his call or message, using the internet to see us and video call to check on everyone, it was lovely, and he loves doing good and acting on it. I spent my life with him, and I won't stop writing about him, and it won't be enough to describe my loss, my burning heart. Yesterday, 10/7/2024, at 7 a.m., he sent a message through Messenger, asking us to call him, and sending messages and calls, and we spoke to him and asked him to come to the south when the army allowed movement from the north to the south, and he strongly refused. He disappeared for a while at noon, and we were all gathered in a yard between tents. My mother and sisters and all my family suddenly got a call from my cousin, asking my mother to speak, and without realizing it I screamed and lost consciousness without understanding. My brother Fadi took the phone and spoke to the caller, and said only Osama. He collapsed to the ground, unconscious. My sisters and his wife screamed and cried, I held myself together, refusing to believe this was happening, this couldn't be, we're one soul, inseparable. I lied to myself; the heartache lasted. I called my cousin to explain what happened, he said he was hit by a scouting missile while riding his bike to school where my relatives were displaced, to give them some ice-cold water. I asked about his condition; he said he was fine but lost his legs and hands. I asked for his son's number, who was in the north with my brother, so I could call and reassure my soul. I called him, and he told me he was in the operating room. My mother screamed that he lost his foot but he was awake, thanking God a thousand times. I said to lift him for life. The important thing is for him to stay. I asked him to keep calling every moment, and I made many calls to my uncles, friends, aunts, wife's people, and everyone I know in the north to go to the hospital and bring me the news, so I could calm the people there and tell them to calm down and pray and wait. I looked at all their faces and felt even more afraid. He can't leave; he's impossible. Don't do it, Osama, and where are you going? This is what I repeated in my head. The calls of condolence began pouring in, and I shouted at the callers that he was fine, still in surgery. I couldn't believe he'd leave us in moments. I ran away into a tent and my heart and body trembled. My cousin called, but I didn't answer until a moment later. "May God give you strength," he said. I said, "What are you talking about? He's in surgery." I screamed his name, my heart exploding, and returned to the screaming, and everyone collapsed crying and rushed to understand what had happened. People gathered in our tent, and my sisters and mother lost consciousness, and my father cried, not believing it. They tried to hug me; I refused, it was impossible, he hadn't left. I kept shouting, unaware, I started running outside, calling Osama. They stopped me from leaving the tent, and I screamed "Lies, he'll call." He was talking to me. The news arrived via Telegram, saying he was martyred. I slapped my face, involuntarily, screaming they published news of his death, he really left. My tears didn't stop; my heart burned; I couldn't console anyone easily. I know he's happy now, sleeping and comfortable. He deserves paradise for what he did and offered. He deserves paradise, and everything beautiful. Everyone remembers him for good news and kind acts. He always advised me about his wife and son, the only things left of him in this world. It's frightening what life will be like without Osama. Few words, lengthy explanation. My beloved has departed. He deserves paradise. Let's meet in paradise.

Fri, July 12 05:21 AM

Audio: [very low, slow, sad voice] "Hello, how are you, I wish you are okay."

06:24 AM

Audio: "Hey, Amira. I just woke up, looked at your message, listened to it. But before I listened, I was already thinking about you. I was already thinking about you this morning. Amira, I just want to let you know how many of us are behind you. We cannot take away your pain, we cannot take away the loss of this beautiful human. But many of us love you and are supporting you, and are thinking about you every day."

06:54 AM

Thank you for everything

07:24 AM

Sun, July 14 06:45 AM

Audio: "Hello Amira . . . let me hear from you. I have been thinking about you every day. Thinking about you, your family, Osama, all of you. You are on my mind. I am hearing the news about Gaza, I know it's very, very bad, and I am hoping that you are okay."

Audio: "We are fine, everyone fine. We are very sad, very lonely, but trying to be okay. Trying to be safe. The situation here is so bad. Nothing is good. The bombing, explosions everywhere. Yesterday in Gaza it was so bad, lose many people. They killed and murdered the people who was in Khan Younis, the place that they say is safety. Eh, we don't know what will happen, we don't know what will we do. But I was thinking of many things to do it for Osama in the north, for the, for the [inaudible], but I don't know, I don't know, but we should do many things. We are okay. Thank you for thinking of us. Thank you for supporting us, thank you for everything. We all love you. Thanks Jeannie, thanks."

07:14 AM

Thank you.

07:45 AM

Audio: *"Me who should thank you for everything. Thank God I have a person and friend like you in my life. That makes me very strong, makes me so happy, someone I can tell him everything. Someone ask me and care about me and my family. That's . . . uh, that's a thing so big, so different, so beautiful for me."*

07:50 AM

Audio: *"I admire you to the ends of the earth Amira. You are wonderful, you really are. And many people are following you and loving you now."*

Audio: *"Do you know what? For many days I want to tell you I am strong. I feel so proud when I listen about Osama and what he do for the people, from other people, whom I don't know, who I cannot see them any days. He didn't tell me what he do for the people. He was go for many places, looking for water, for food, and give it for them. He cannot eat alone. He thinking, with everyone around him. I'm so proud that my brother was a good man for many. A good brother, a good friend, a good husband. He is, how I can say that . . . he is like a miracle. He deserves the heaven. I will be sad for all my life to lose him. My heart is pain. I cannot imagine the day when we come back for the home and we cannot find him, or see him, or hug him. Many things, thinking of it is so hard, so difficult. But I want to continue what he was [doing]. I want to be proud all the time with him. I want to listen and talk about him for all the world to know Osama, know what he was doing, and know that he is not guilty, I don't know, but thank God I have a friend, brother, a love like Osama. Thanks."*

08:27 AM

Audio: "We will spread the word about Osama. You can be sure about that."

Mon, July 15 09:13 AM

Audio: "How are you, I wish you are okay. I was speaking for Osama's friend; her name is Valaria from Argentina but [she lives] in Spain. She was know him from 2018 from when he was injured at the border. She send me many posts that he send for her. We don't have it. In Khan Younis, the first time we see it. And for that I think to look for many memories for Osama and ask her what she have. [Laughter.] I laugh because everyone is looking [at] me I don't know for why . . . but, I like that so much."

09:48 AM

Audio: "Hi, Amira, this is great news. I would love to see some of the posts that he sent. I think that what you're saying is that this woman Valaria has many posts from Osama. Things that he sent her, things that he wrote, and that she is giving them to you. So if this is what you're saying, I would love to see some of these beautiful posts. I would love to. If you would share those, I would be very happy. Thank you, love you. It was great to hear you laugh. Great to hear you laugh. I'm so happy to hear that."

10:45–10:53 AM

Photos of Osama (37A, 37B, 37C, and 37D): his baby son, his mom, just Osama, and the March of Return, 2018.

04:27 PM

Photos 37E, 37F, and 37G: many people gathered around a water tank truck with large bright-yellow and dark-blue water jugs.

This was the distribution of free drinking water to the displaced people in a school, a shelter center in the city of Beit Hanoun, north of Gaza, as a mercy to the soul of Osama. He lived in the school with them and tried to provide them with food and drink.

Wed, July 17 06:20 PM

My phone broke! I'm sorry. I just got it back

I was completely out of touch with everyone.

Thu, July 18 04:24 AM

Oh sorry to hear that, the important thing is that you are okay

I am ok and still with you every day.

09:57 AM

Roland has submitted the book to a few publishing agents and is waiting to hear back. However, this week I am getting back to work. I will add the current events.

I feel I am now racing to finish and perhaps self-publish.

10:56 AM

Do you know, for a while I completely forgot about it, but now I am very determined for it to end and spread so that everyone knows Osama was with me in the events from the beginning, and I want everyone to remember him.

I feel this way almost exactly. The difference is I want them to know you as well.

Audio: "To be honest, that was the idea from the first time [for] this book. That if anything happen for me, if I don't survive from this war, this book will be remembered all over

the world, and everyone will know Amira. Now, everyone will know who is Osama. And he don't survive. Maybe that is my destiny, I don't know, we don't survive—[child crying in background, an adult scolds]—but I want everyone, every human in this world to know his story."

Audio: "Sorry for the noise. My brother Mohammad was fighting with my little sister. His voice is low . . . high. Sorry sorry."

Sat, July 20, 02:20 PM

Are you there?

03:15 PM

Hi yes, I'm here now

Ok, thank you. Checking in with you.

I am at work, happy for your response

4:17 PM

I wish the best for you all the time

05:09 PM

The same. Thinking about you often.

Mon, July 22 05:42 AM

Hi Amira. Thinking of you.

Audio: "Good evening, dear, how are you? I wish you are okay. I'm trying to be fine. Not so easy, but, uh, thanks for God for everything. When I thinking of Osama, my heart, I feel pain so hard. I crying. I cannot imagine I will not see him another time, and he go. The truth that he go, I don't know how I can believe that, but he go. [Big sigh.] How are you and what are you doing? The situation here is so bad, so difficult, very hard. Hope everything will be fine soon."

Audio: "Hi Amira. I am okay. It's very early in the morning here. I just woke up and realized that I didn't hear from you for a couple days, so I wanted to see how you were. I know that your heart is heavy, and broken, and that it's hard. I hear it in your voice, how difficult it is. My very good friend Rain, her name is Rain, her younger brother was killed in a car accident last week. It's the same thing, the sadness is just so great. I have never lost a brother or sister yet. We're all old, and [small laugh] and we're all still here. I cannot imagine having lost them when I was so young. I can't imagine this pain. I am just so very sorry. I know that he meant the world to you. I know that he was the one that stood for you. I know he was the one that protected you when he could. I know he was beautiful, handsome, strong, and that he was another superhero. Someone who gave everything. He took the risk to help other people, and I'm, I'm just very sorry that this is all happening. I don't understand why, and I don't understand God's ways, what the plan is. But the world is still speaking up for Palestine. My son Roland is coming tomorrow to be with me, and I'm very happy for that. But yes, I am thinking about you very much, and I love you, Amira."

Photo 37A

Photo 37B

Photo 37C

Photo 37D

Photo 37E

Photo 37F

Photo 37G

CHAPTER 38
WHO WILL MAKE A DIFFERENCE

I can't say a person is good unless they have the opportunity to do evil and don't. You must have choices to truly know who you are. My visible scars mean I was stronger than what they tried to hurt me.

06:36 AM

Audio: I am so happy to know that Roland will come tomorrow and visit you. That makes me so happy and make me think you will have a good and beautiful time. Our loss, it is not easy. It is very difficult, very hard. I cannot imagine how I can come back from the north without, uh, how I cannot see him anymore. He lose his life, yes. I was thinking about that next day, after the war, how it will be. When I hug him, see him, speak with him, sharing our speak and laugh, everything we will share. But now . . . I don't know. To be honest, I don't know how to be thinking about that. But I'm sure he's in a better place. He deserve the heaven. [Deep sigh.] He was all of my world, my heart, my friend, my love, my everything. The pain will not go. The pain, my heart will be broken all my life. I will do what I can for his son. I will do what I can to be a person that he will love to see him, as he want. [Sigh.] We heard the news that a woman will, I don't know how to say that, in

America, Harris, that's what's [her] name. I don't understand what will be different, I don't understand what she will do for us. But I wish that change will come very soon. A good change. The positive change. The war will finish. That's what we need. Certainly. Just that. Stop killing the people, stop making mistake [inaudible] in Gaza. Now today, the situation in Khan Younis is so hard. They arrive, the people who was in east of Gaza, to arrive from their home and their place, to another place. We don't know what will happen."

09:53 AM

I hear your pain. The pain of Gaza is in your voice.

Kamala Harris is the Vice President of the United States. She will now be running for president because Joe Biden dropped out.

Audio: "We know that from the news. But we ask . . . What . . . Will . . . She . . . Do. She will be the best choice? Or bad or worse than others. Who knows. You know that is the first time that a woman will be as a president. It's so different, so, I don't know. For us here, in Arab exactly, I cannot imagine. But I hope she will be better than others."

I understand. I don't know if she will be better.

We will see. We are still hoping for a better choice. I don't know how strong she is.

Audio: "This exactly what I mean. She should be very strong woman to be president and do the better thing for everyone. To be the better choice."

10:33 AM

Audio: "I'm sure she is very strong in many ways. However, I do not know if she is strong enough to stand up to the Zionist machine. This is what I mean. As a young girl, she would go out and collect money for making the desert bloom. Because since she was a little girl she was told, you know, that Israel was . . . she was educated the wrong way, and I don't know if she can see the truth. And this is what I'm saying about her. Yeah, she's smart, yeah, she's strong, but she's maybe not ethically and morally strong enough, and I think there will be a lot of pressure on her. The reason Roland is coming to see me is because Netanyahu is coming to Washington and we are going to participate in a very big protest. There will be tens of hundreds of thousands of people surrounding the capital. and that's what we're doing Wednesday."

10:37 AM

Audio: "The only thing that I want to say is we, from heart, thank all the people who stand behind us, thinking of us, supporting us, do that for us, thinking of Palestine and Palestinian. And who knows? We hope everything will change when this war ends. Or any person can change anything, as a little, for us. We hope."

Audio: "I agree with you. That change and hope come from unexpected places. It seems like, oh, will Kamala help us? But I think the hope is going to come from somewhere that is not expected. And this is what I'm waiting for. Not waiting, but this is what I am looking forward to."

Yes exactly 100%.

11:14 AM

O friend who grew within my ribs,

I shared my soul with him, so he became its intimate companion.

How could you leave me alone in this world?

I search for your eyes among the passers-by but do not find them.

Your apparition never leaves my thoughts for a moment,

Followed by tears leaving their sockets.

I miss you as one misses death, bitter and acrid,

My solace and my heart's patience are that you are in a deserving paradise.

Healing for my soul is a meeting and an embrace in my dreams,

Making me repeat: "If only we could repeat it in the eternal abode."

11:15 AM

Wow. Yes.

Wed, July 24 10:39 AM

Headed out with Roland to March for Palestine. Praying for you and all.

Thanks so much 🙏

12:54 PM

Photo 38A: Jeannie and Roland during the March in Washington, DC, protesting the arrival of war criminal Netanyahu.

Wow so beautiful 🤗 thanks for everything

01:18 PM

We love you

Me to love you so much

Fri, July 26 03:15 PM

Hi Amira, I am checking in on you.

04:53 PM

Hi dear I'm fine what about you for sorry that internet so bad

05:39 PM

I am ok. I'm keeping track of you when possible

Sat, July 27 02:10 AM

Mon, July 29 03:09 AM

Good morning how are you

Sorry for asking about this, but I need urgent help, as things here are very difficult, and I have not received my volunteer salary for the third month, and conditions are very bad.

05:14 AM

Ok.

05:30 AM

Tue, July 30 06:49 PM

I will have funds in 2 days.

10:14 PM

Oh thank you so much

You are welcome.

Wed, July 31 06:44 AM

Audio: *"Good evening, dear how are you? I wish you are okay. Thank you, thank you for everything. I am thinking of you all the time, but for the—sorry, the internet connection, it was so bad for almost all of the day. For that we are still here in Khan Younis, Asdaa City. Ehh . . . wish the situation will be better, the war will finish very soon."*

07:05 AM

So glad, as always, to hear your voice.

07:22 AM

Audio: *"Happy to know that you are okay and fine. Trying to move in this life. You know we cannot stop. We cannot do anything, we just continue to survive, continue to be safe, continue to have a life. A normal life [small laugh], as we can."*

Photo 38A

CHAPTER 39
AID

Stress changes a person in a terrifying way. You find traits in them that are neither like them nor similar to them. You may see them as fierce despite their kindness, evil despite their kindness, or unjust despite their justice. How many people have had their white hearts stained by the blackness of night, losing themselves and everyone around them because of their struggle with the harshness of the days and their helplessness due to their agitation and excitement over everything.

لي

07:08 AM

Please tell me how much aid is getting in if you know. Also, how are you buying food? How are the markets getting their supplies? We hear many different reports. Can you explain as best you can how all of this is working?

07:22 AM

Audio: "About that, I just want to ask, which aids exactly? To know how I can answer about that. Buying food, here in the market in Gaza, it's so expensive, and many things are not found here. From where we get it, it comes from the West Bank to Gaza, to buy it and get it in many ways."

I do not know exactly the amount of aid.

As for obtaining food, we no longer receive food aid due to the closure of the Rafah crossing, from which it used to arrive. It now enters Gaza. Only the trucks and commercial goods that fill the markets by merchants come from the West Bank through the Kerem Shalom crossing and are very expensive, as they exploit the people's needs, but there are no other alternatives. We are forced to buy and obtain

Yes, I mean the food. Is all the food coming and being taken to be sold?

Do you know that I go out during the dawn hours to get drinking water? Sometimes I stand for a long time among large numbers of women, there is crowding and crowding, we receive violent blows, and we get wet with water, which we get through with great suffering, as most of the water available is not suitable for drinking.

Yes, exactly. No aid here to people after they close Rafah. They just sold in marketing, and sold as expensive, as usual. Some things come from the north when the Jewish open the route behind the north and the south. Some people get some, sells, from there. We cannot find the clean...

We cannot find sanitary ware, shampoo, soap, etc. in the market, and what is available is very expensive

I know you must buy your supplies. I hear that many aid trucks are attacked by settlers or blocked from entry. I wonder if some merchants are still buying their supplies and these are the trucks coming in.

Netanyahu said they have sent 40,000 aid trucks, which were all attacked by armed Hamas and stolen. I think he is lying about some of it. But it seems some aid is being stolen. Yes, we hear about the lack of sanitary supplies, esp. for women.

We heard that Israel recently blew up another water source.

We hear that people are dying of starvation in the north.

This is true, the north suffers from famine and lack of sources of food and drink, but it contains factories of cleaning supplies and soap. The center is considered Gaza City, so it has some deficiencies in the south. When the road was opened, some people coming from the north to the south to escape hunger brought with them some sanitary tools to sell to obtain money that they did not have. To buy other supplies, they were sold at a very high price due to their lack of availability and the intense need for them.

As for what is mentioned, after the closure of the Rafah crossing, no aid entered Gaza, only some commercial trucks for sale and filled the markets, all of which are Palestinian products from the cities of the West Bank and some other Arab and Turkish countries. We do not know if it is aid and is being sold in the market, as this has happened many times before.

True, some trucks are attacked and blown up and some are killed. Other than that, there are some people who intercept them out of extreme hunger.

Thank you for explaining. This makes complete sense.

CHAPTER 40
HOW WILL THE FIRST DAY BE?

Mahmoud, there is nothing left on this earth worth living for.

There is no longer anything called life.

On this land, death, destruction, blood and violence surround us from all sides.

Fear has settled on our pillows and loomed over our nights... Our dreams have been stolen and assassinated in cold blood. They broke our hearts and extinguished our spirits, Mahmoud. They have placed a barrier between us and the life we deserve. Everything has become faded, the colors of the walls, the streets, the clouds, the sounds, the music, the buildings, the cars. Everything is faded, silent, and frightening, still, the silence of death... The mother of the martyr undulates in grief over who she has said goodbye to, and another cries over her wounded blood, and a child trembles in terror, having lost his source of livelihood, not knowing where to start, and the falafel seller is sad, and the bookstore owner is sick, and the children curse the occupation a thousand times. How will that rubble be replaced and the ashes removed? We left everything behind us for an unknown destination.

And here we are beseeching God to have mercy on us with His mercy,
to restore to us what our souls have lost, or we are waiting for our
turn to become stories that are told and narrated. We are searching
for some peace and security. Our hearts are terrified by the shocks.
We beseech God not to burden us with what we cannot bear. Is it a
nightmare that will end? Or will our wait be prolonged?

Sat, August 3 02:48 PM

Audio: "Dear, good evening, how are you today? I'm sorry I
wasn't connected with you the last day, but you know the
internet connection was so bad. To be honest with you, I was
thinking about the last day, when Roland sent the post of
Osama and Batool, the child, my cousin. I was really really
thinking about what will happen on the day after the war,
when it finish, end, stop. How we will continue our life. Okay, I
know that we can stop and take our breath. We are surviving.
We are not numbers. Everyone had a story to tell the world
about it. But I don't know. Will our life come back as normal
as it was? I cannot imagine that."

04:47 PM

This is difficult to answer. Your life will never go back as it was. You know that. How it will go is unknown. Your life has become a survival of one minute to the next, saturated with grief and uncertainty. How will the world respond when it is the moment to rebuild Gaza. You will not be rebuilding just stones and tile, archways, gardens, streets, and orchards. You are rebuilding your spirits and minds, your will to live, reclaiming the best of your culture amidst tremendous odds. It is not a task to be done alone. While some of the world chooses to remain steeped in ignorance, much of the world is becoming willing to help. How the help will arrive, God knows. I don't know what the light is at the end of this war. I just believe there is one.

To all of you who show courage, strength, who still get up at dawn to search for water, scour the markets, hug the children, and feel that the ache for your murdered family members will never disappear, feel that even in your suffering and grief, we are looking up to you. None of us knows what we can endure. Not even you. Most of us would be begging for mercy and forgetting the word hope. But you, you still go out in the dawn for water. You are a miracle of God.

04:54 PM

Audio: [speaking quietly, inaudible] ". . . speaking with you, I'm sure about that. Our life, it's continue. If we survive, if we had . . . alive when this war will finish, it stop, ended. The day, the next day after this war will be so difficult, so hard. Our heart will have pain. Maybe we can cry. I don't know, I don't know what will we do. But I thinking about, come back for a normal life, it's so impossible. I thinking about, when this war will finish, many thing we lose. Not just many thing. We lose everything. We lose people that we are love them so much, and I cannot imagine my life without them. We lose our houses. We lose Gaza. We lose certainly a year from our life. We day after day lose many things. We trying to take our breath, we trying to survive. We trying to continue as we can, and be strongly. But who know? Sometimes I feel that I don't have any power to do anything. I don't have power to be sad, crying, to say for anyone that I'm here. I'm not okay. You understand me, I know that. Everything in the future is unknown for us exactly. Maybe we are still alive, we survive, maybe we . . . cannot. I'm here now, after a minute, but who know? But it's very hard thinking about, if I'm still alive, the day, the next day from this war will be the worse. The worst from forever. For this war at all. I guess that I cannot, I feel that . . . people who die, they are survive. But we, but we are not. But who are still alive, he doesn't survive. He lose all his life. He lose everything. He is not in a life. I don't know, and I don't understand, but that is the true. Who go, who die, he survive from this bad day. From this bad war, from this bad, I don't know how I can describe this situation, but it is very hard. Thinking of that fill me that time I fall down, cannot wake up, cannot stand up. But I should! I should be! I should stand up. I should be trying to continue the day, trying to continue to be okay, trying to get a good thing, as I can."

The end of the war as the most difficult day? Yes, I understand. This will be the day you will look and feel all the loss and ask yourself and the world…Now what? Now what?

05:14 PM

Audio: "Yes, exactly, that's what I think about. Now what? When we come back and build Gaza again. Build everything that they destroy it. Who will get back who we love, who we lose. Who will get back the day we are travelling from place to place, escaping, trying to be safety, trying to survive. Get back the day we should be as a normal life. Our work, our places, our families, our houses. Many things. Who will get back this thing. And if it's back, who will back the people who we lose, who they murder. I don't know. After that, what? Really. What?"

I don't have an answer. All I can promise is that I will still be here, my family and some friends, we will stay the course for you. My son Roland, my friend Michael, they are strong and they are committed. You will not be alone.

05:47 PM

Audio: "I know that I'm not alone. I'm sure that you are with me all the time. And I thank you, and thanks all the friends who are thinking of me and [yawn] think of all Palestinians here in Gaza. I will be happy, as I am proud to know you and have a friend like you. One day, if I survive, if I have a life, to meet you and thank you face to face, and hug you. Maybe I can, then I will cry from my heart. I'm sure. I'm sure that when I feel that I'm, I feel when I need for some help for somebody to stand behind me I will find you. Thank you so much. I love you so much. I love that you are my friends."

06:33 PM

I hear in your voice that you are in the sleep time, but you are not sleeping.

Amira, it is I that is incredibly honored and proud to know you.

06:52 PM

Me to so proud to have a friend like you

You are a Superhero. And Osama is a Superhero. He is still there for you. Maybe he died because he knew that he would be by your side, and Hassan's side, always.

ACKNOWLEDGMENTS

From Amira

Amira dedicates this book to her brother Osama.

From Jeannie

With an enormous amount of gratitude to those who were with me along this journey, never wavering in their faith in this project and exhibiting endless patience, especially with me.

My children, Justin, Kima, and Roland

Michael Leonardi, Patrick Dennis, and Lori Nunnely

Editor and interior designer Abbie Phelps

Cover designer Manlio Pertout

Logo designer Martha Stephens

All of the powerful people speaking for Palestine